A Memoir
of Love, Loss
and Life

Life
AFTER
LOSSES

James LaVeck

Text: James LaVeck (www.jameslaveck.com)
Editor: Mary Rakow, Ph.D. (www.maryrakow.com)
Cover Design: Danielle Smith-Boldt
Interior Design and Layout: Danielle Smith-Boldt

ISBN: 978-1-7357707-0-3 (paperback)
      978-1-7357707-1-0 (hardcover)
      978-1-7357707-2-7 (ebook)

# DEDICATIONS

*For Robert John Roders:*  *You taught me how to love, and how to be loved. You proved that I could love, and was good enough to be loved. Unconditionally.*

*For Robert Harold Meek-LaVeck:*  *You taught me to live again, and proved I could love more than one person in my lifetime. You gave me your love and accepted my broken-hearted past.*

*For Troy:*  *You opened my eyes to the possibility of loving and being loved again, for which I'll always be thankful.*

*For Richard:*  *You, too, opened my eyes that I was worthy of being loved, despite my baggage. Timing and geography left me wondering, "what if?"*

*For Mom:*  *You have supported me throughout my life, comforting, advising, and always loving. You taught me how to be who I am, to be independent, to be a hard-worker, and to provide for my family.*

*For Abby:*  *You opened my heart to the possibility of being a dad, and have provided me with unconditional love that I never expected to have in my life.*

**For Daniel:** *You made my heart grow larger from the moment I held you, showing that the capacity to love is never-ending.*

**For Wanda:** *You accepted me immediately; you accepted our children the moment they came into our lives. To this day, you provide love and support for which I am eternally grateful.*

**For Jessy:** *You started as my boss, but wound up being a dear friend to both Bobs. One of the few friends that bridged them both and one we chose to take care of our children if anything were to happen to us. Thank you for being there.*

**For all of you that entered my life:** *You are part of my history, part of who I am and part of my story. Whether you are currently part of my life and circle of influence or you were, I am thankful for the lessons I have learned from you, both the good and the bad experiences.*

**And finally, for the Reader:** *You inspire me and I hope my story inspires you as you journey toward healing and finding your new life after loss.*

*This book is not intended to be a how-to book for dealing with grief, however. There are many books from professionals that can help you with that, and I've read several of them. I am not a licensed grief counselor.*

*Instead, this book is a memoir of my life, which includes losing two husbands before I was 48 years old. I wrote this book from a place of honesty and an open heart. My wish is that you find this a story of hope. At the risk of sounding cliche, it is a story about learning to pick yourself up when life knocks you down, and pushing ahead when your forward momentum is interrupted by a brick wall.*

*This story shares what worked for me, and importantly, those the things I did, that in hindsight, prevented me from picking myself up. It's a bit of a "lessons learned" from a flawed human being to you, Dear Reader.*

*I invite you to join us at http://lifeafterlosses.com for more conversations.*

# CONTENTS

## Chapter One
# MY FIRST HUSBAND

## PROLOGUE I

His skin is yellow. A result of the damage to his liver. His hair is thinner than when I first met him, seven and a half years ago. The result of the chemotherapy. His face and body are skeletal. A body that served him well for nearly 36 years. A body that held me close, kept me warm, and excited me. A body that is now in the process of shutting down. A body that bounced back time and again. But it would not bounce back now. Not this time. The doctor said the disease was terminal, "Didn't anyone tell you?" he asked. No, we weren't prepared for this. I am not prepared for this.

My Mom is here, too, helping. I am holding his hand, Mom's doing dishes, and I hear a sound from Bob that I'd not heard before. "It's time," I call out to her, knowing we are at the end. We are both holding a hand, telling him "It's okay. You can leave whenever you're ready."

I say, "It's okay, honey," but I don't mean it. He knows. In the moment of that last breath, the one I would remember, that would haunt my dreams, he squeezes our hands as we hear one final gasp. Is it a sign that he is okay with this? Is it a sign to give us strength when we would need it most? Is it a sign of pain? Is it the last-ditch effort of a dying man grasping to take something with him? Or is he trying to hold onto this world and to us?

Then it is over. His grip relaxes on our hands. His eyes stare heavenward.

I've now learned that death is not peaceful.

For a moment, it is only me, my Mother, and Bob. Silent. Tears stream down my face, my body is wracked with grief, a mewling sound I'd never heard escapes my mouth, and then an instantaneous numbing to what is occurring around me. I'm aware of my Mother's crying. She brings me a glass of wine to help calm me. It won't be the last. I know she is hurting, too, I just can't seem to get beyond my own pain, my own disbelief, to help comfort her. I need to make phone calls. I know that if I stop for just a second, I won't be able to pick myself up.

I'm thankful when the visiting nurse arrives. She and Mom are in the bathroom with all of the medication, flushing the toilet. I hear this, but I don't. Bob's cousin arrives. We hug, we cry. She had been so helpful over the last five months—just about as long as I had known her. She helped my Mom take care of Bob during the final three weeks of his life. All of our friends, his friends, visited, saying goodbye. We laughed and cried together, and, for a time, it actually seemed that Bob was getting better. Could a miracle be on the way? Will he live and be cured? The events of today tell me "no." In fact, it was a false hope but we needed something to believe in. I tried God. He didn't answer as I thought He should. How could He let Bob suffer like that? What was this I heard about a merciful and loving God? I couldn't believe it true. The God I know wouldn't allow people to suffer like this.

"You can't have a rose without thorns," Father David Carriere says four days later, presiding over the memorial service. I am still numb. I hear the words but don't. Soon, I will have to speak. I have asked David Blackmore and Gillian Wilson, two of Bob's oldest friends, to speak. I asked Jack, our new neighbor in the house we bought less than a year ago. Jack and Bob became quick friends. Jack and Tere, his wife, and their daughters, Christine and Cynthia, invited us to their home for Easter. We enjoyed their company; we enjoyed playing games with their kids in our front yard. They were each drawn to Bob, as I was, for his wit and ability to make us laugh. There was just something about him that made him get along with anyone and everyone. He had a way of putting a person at ease, of making one feel comfortable in his presence. Some "Christians" would say that Bob and I got what we deserved for the supposed sin of loving each other. I don't remember hate being taught by Christ.

Father David is almost finished. I know I will have to hear David, Gill, and Jack speak before I get up and say what I need to say. Or, more likely, what I think I should say for the 75 or so people gathered here to remember him, to offer me comfort, to let me comfort them. I'm not sure I can handle it, but the numbness, the shock of it all, will get me through this.

I am also upset that Bob's only brother didn't make it. He's always been a flake. I know the stress he caused his father and his brother. I am also upset that only one member of Bob's family came. My entire family is here. Even my brother, with whom I've been estranged for some time. And friends that neither of us had seen in a while. Even some of my co-workers and Bob's co-workers are here. Why couldn't his family be here? This is for Bob as much as it is for me. Fellowship in man and all that.

Father David is wrapping up. As I write this, I no longer remember who is first, Jack, David, or Gill. I only know that soon I will speak. I hear the music I chose to be played as the speakers eulogize. This was the music Bob was listening to as he died. A cut from the *Saltimbanco* CD by Cirque du Soleil. Somewhere in my mind, removed from reality, I hear Gillian speak of Bob's journey in life and into the next. I hear her say that there is a thread that holds us together, "Bob hasn't dropped his end, he has just taken it around the corner."

Oh, God, what am I doing here?!? Why am I here? Soon, I will speak, I will ask that another song be played when I am done. A song that, to this day, brings tears to my eyes and touches something deep inside me. If it weren't for this song, we would be holding the memorial services at a Catholic Church. I'm not sure why, but holding the service in Church is something Bob had asked for but didn't insist on. I told him I wanted this song played.

After his death, Mom and I went to the funeral director and told him what we wanted for the service, including music. He tried with the church, but they wouldn't allow any "non-liturgical music with no meaning" played. They insisted that we have an organist, even though I didn't want one. I was crushed. Screw the church, I thought. Let's have the service here at the Funeral Home.

I guess it's time for me to speak now. I squeeze my Mother's hand, my rock ever near, and paste a smile on my face. I wander up to the podium with my notes in hand. Am I going to be able to do this? My hands are trembling. God, there are so many people here. I know how to do public speaking, but this is different. I clear my throat. I unfold my notes. I begin,

> *"When Bob was first diagnosed with cancer in March, we didn't quite know where to turn. We found the Living With Cancer Support Group at CMH, and within a few weeks, we met Sally and John. John was diagnosed with cancer around the same time as Bob.*
>
> *"I brought Bob home from the hospital three weeks ago, after he was told that he only had a few days left. I called Sally the next day to tell her that he'd come home. She told me that John had just passed away earlier that day.*
>
> *"I spoke with Sally a few days later, and she told me that John's services were going to*

be a celebration of John's life because, as she said, his life was 57 years and his death was only one day. I thought that was beautiful. I mentioned it to Bob, and he said that's what he wanted. A party. A celebration of his 35 years on this earth. A celebration of how he touched us all. So that's what we're doing.

"As I am sure you know from reading the memorial cards that were passed out with Bob's picture, we are celebrating his life, and a form of celebration is dancing.

"In a way, Bob wound up dancing with us all. Everyone he came in contact with, even after he got sick, stuck around and continued to dance with him. You hear stories of people who just can't handle being around sick people. But we didn't experience any of that. Instead, we learned who our true friends were, and we made a few new ones along the way.

"Bob was always thinking of others, treating people with respect (even when they didn't deserve it sometimes). He was worried about me, how I was going to do, how I was going to make it financially with the new house and all. I told him not to worry about me because he made so many of you promise to take care of me.

*"About a week after I brought him home,
he was just so weak. My Mom and I would
help him get out of bed, and I'd have him put
his arms around my neck as I lifted him up.
When we walked or turned around, I told him
that we were just going to do a little dancing.
He continued to use all of his strength to help
us as we helped him. We were with him when
he passed, and even then, he used what little
strength he had to give us a gentle squeeze to
our hands. Even at the moment of death, he
was thinking about others.*

*"I told him about a week ago that I was
having a crisis. I told him that part of me
is glad that we had seven pretty great years
together—some great, some really great, and
some not so great—and that I wouldn't give
that up for anything. Then I said that part of
me would give it up if he could be healthy and
continue to touch people's lives the way he did. I
told him it would be pretty selfish of me to keep
him all to myself when there are so many of you.*

*"The song I am about to have played deals
with this little dance of life we are all doing.
Specifically, the dance we shared with Bob
throughout his life. I'd like you to listen to the
words. If you know it, please sing along. If you
don't, just listen and see what it means to you."*

A few notes from a piano play through the speakers and I hear Garth Brooks' *The Dance.* Time to be numb again, fight back any tears; somehow, find my way back to my seat. *"Our lives are better left to chance. I could have missed the pain, but I'd have had to miss The Dance."* We'll be home soon for the requisite gathering. Somehow, I manage to make it out of the building. I see a lot of people, I hug a lot of people, and I speak with everyone, though I don't really hear a thing.

Back at the house, many people arrive. Most bring food. Why is it that when someone dies, people bring food? I am thankful because I probably won't cook anything, and I guess I need to eat. We laugh, remembering some of the silly things Bob did. His brother shows up. What the hell is he doing here? Couldn't make it to his own brother's memorial service, but now he's here. I make it through the rest of the day and into the evening.

Everyone's gone now, except for my brother and my Mom. I let go of myself. I don't like the feeling. It hurts so much. The coming days are a blur. There is a Bereavement Support Group meeting in a few days. I think I need to go.

I bring Mom with me to grieve with others who are suffering some type of loss. She would stay with me a number of weeks, and attend with me, before she would go back home. I am the youngest one there. I am also the only one that lost a lover of the same sex. It doesn't seem to matter. The Group accepts me; my loss is as real as theirs. Most of them are mourning their spouse. So am I. I come to depend on these people. We have nothing in common but our common losses, and we build on that. We build friendships, companionship, and fellowship. It is here that Roni, our facilitator, puts the idea in my head to write a journal. To take the emotions I have and let them out, to put them on paper.

I wrote the preceding words in 1997, two years after his death. It would become a prologue to what would become a 250-page book of journal entries and musings of the first three years after Bob's death. It would become part of my journey to healing and recovery. I've learned much more about this journey, and myself, since August 14, 1995.

## A Life-Altering Meeting

We met in early 1988. I had been living with my sister Karen, or her with me, since moving to Santa Barbara for University. She was about to be married, and I needed to find a roommate. Santa Barbara is gorgeous but expensive. As a 21-year-old, I was just getting comfortable in my sexuality and wanted to find a roommate with whom I could be my authentic self. To that end, I went to our local Gay & Lesbian Resource Center to look at the bulletin board for people looking for roommates. I figured it would be much easier to live my authentic self in a household where others were like me.

I found an ad that spoke to me, a room in a house on the west side of Santa Barbara with one gay man and a woman. It was a single-story bungalow-style home located behind another with a shared carport between the two buildings. The outside was painted a chocolate brown, night-blooming jasmine climbing a trellis, and it had a porch on which one could sit and chat. Inside, the walls were adorned with knotted pine tongue-in-groove panels and a big window facing the carport. Along the wall opposite the front door hung half of a dead Christmas tree. A sofa separated the living from the dining area.

When I knocked on the door to interview, Bob was doing dishes, an apron tied around his waist. Brown hair, sparkling blue eyes, with a beard and a smile that could melt the ice caps. He was 7 years my senior, I was barely 21 and sowing my oats at the local bars. We went through the interview process and looked at what would become my bedroom and the back yard. I met Scout, the Golden Retriever that was nicknamed "Speed Bump." He had an uncanny ability to just flop down in front of people wanting to go somewhere, forcing them to slow down to step over him. I felt comfortable enough to accept the offer and to provide references to my new potential roommate.

A number of months later, we realized that he'd already witnessed one of the pivotal moments of my life when I came to accept who I was and how I was made.

## My Story

I was the middle-child product of a marriage between an American GI and a German citizen that met while my father was stationed in Wiesbaden Germany in the late

1950s. We were a typical middle-class family. My sister Karen was born in 1962, I followed four years later, and my brother Chris three years after that. Mom, dad, three kids, suburban neighborhood; we started off Catholic, my parents and sister moving from New York State to Southern California before my birth.

I don't remember much about those early years, though one of my first memories was watching my father pack up his bar glasses. He was moving out. In hindsight, I think it telling the earliest memory I have is him packing up his bar glasses–and that he felt the need to pack them to leave. His excessive drinking was a major factor in my Mother's decision to divorce in 1970. I was just under four-years-old, my sister was eight and our brother was nine months old by the time the divorce was final; I was told the Church no longer let my Mom attend services as a divorcee.

The years following had the three of us kids shuffled between two households, though it was clear my younger brother and I didn't want anything to do with our father and his new wife. She punished my brother for eating the last banana and once fed him dog food. She was a heavy drinker herself.

In 4th grade, I realized I had a crush on one of my teachers, one that happened to be a man. It was a far more intense feeling that when Vanessa pulled me aside, in my short seersucker suit and bow tie, during her 5th Birthday party to give me a kiss. I was shocked, and assumed the butterflies in my stomach was from all the sugar in the ice cream sundaes.

In late 1978/early 1979, my Mother had an opportunity to move us out of the Los Angeles area. I was 12, my sister was 16, attracting all the wrong boys and attention, according to Mom. My Mom thought it best to move to a rural location in the high desert around the Sequoia National Park. We had vacationed in the area many times and enjoyed it, so the kids agreed that it would be a good move away from the city. That was also the last time I saw my father in person. He dropped us off at our new home in February 1979 and dropped out of our lives. I don't remember crying.

Being gay in America in the 1980s was difficult, especially for a kid going through middle and high school in a rural area. I had 111 in my graduating class. We were bombarded with the news of AIDS killing gays, always reminded that we would be dead by the time we were 25. We were told it was God's punishment. It took six years into the epidemic for our President to even utter the word "AIDS." He didn't consult medical sources for a course of action; he reached out to the leaders of the religious right. It was a clear message to us that we were expendable.

Now, growing up in a conservative, rural area, it was hard to avoid the religion thing. I voluntarily went to a few churches in our town, as I had done before we moved, trying to find the right fit. I wanted to be on the right side of God because I didn't want to die, and I was a good person. I could suppress "the gay" if I had to. I got baptized (again), I attended services and Bible study. I had girlfriends throughout high school, but I also looked at some boys. I was sure I was the only one at my school. I later learned that one of my best friends was gay, but we'd never talked about it.

I was at our childhood friend Dan's wedding and seated at my table was another friend from school. The three of us used to be as thick as thieves, but it would be years after we left High School that we learned each other's secrets. I wonder how less stressful our lives would have been as teenagers to know that we weren't alone.

I did what all my peers did in school. We went to dances, sporting events, bonfires, drinking, smoking, and making out. Some of my peers took that a little further than I did. I had to remind myself I was a good Christian boy. And as I was dating girls, I must've become a magnet of sorts since 5 of the 6 girls I'd dated had confided in me they had been sexually assaulted by the time we met. And as a teenager secretly not heterosexual, it was an excellent excuse to keep things above the clothing.

In 1983, my Mother fell in love and married Jim. I was a Junior in High School when they said their "I Do's" on Thanksgiving Day, when he not only married my Mom, but took on the two teenagers still at home. I was thankful she found a good man to share her life with.

By the time my senior year rolled around, I started dating a girl that lived an hour's drive away. I visited her frequently, and even though she was one of the five, I thought there was a chance we could make each other happy and I began to imagine a future with her. Grad Night 1985, I took her with my class to Disneyland and we spent the night enjoying the rides and our time together. I'd be spending the summer teaching merit badges to Boy Scouts, and I wouldn't get to see her much. Here's where you'd expect the story to take a turn, like falling in love with another counselor and running off into the sunset. That didn't happen. I finished my summer and then prepared to go to college in Santa Barbara.

The University of California at Santa Barbara was the only university to which I applied. I saw the campus, and fell in love with everything about it. Its proximity to the ocean reminded me of the summer heading into my 4th grade. My Mom was managing a motel across the beach in Oceanside, California. We swam nearly all day, and there was a dolphin that would play with us. We learned to surf. The ocean has always been a draw to me. I wouldn't even consider another option. And with a 4.0 GPA, I was confident I wouldn't need a "fall back" school. I didn't.

At the same time I was planning to move, my sister wanted to live in the Santa Barbara area. As with me, the ocean pulls at her and she had friends in the area. We could room together, we thought. I didn't plan on living in the dorms or a fraternity at UCSB, so sharing an apartment might not be a bad idea. We rented an apartment in Goleta. I'd been working since I was 13 and saved most of my money. I didn't qualify for financial aid after my Mother remarried, and I didn't think the responsibility fell on the shoulders of my new step-father. There were 3 of us with 4.0 GPAs in school, so scholarship monies and opportunities were spread out.

One of my first jobs was working for my Mom and her business partner in construction. I wielded a hammer on framing, roofing, and finish work. I helped with insulation and drywall. I became a Jack of all trades with a little bit of knowledge about a lot of different things, enough to be potentially dangerous, I joke.

I did this work alongside my Mom. She was in her mid-40's swinging hammers and picking up framing. This, even after multiple lower-back surgeries. She taught me work ethic. While we were growing up, and my Father failed to pay child support, she made ends meet by working two jobs. When it became impossible to do everything, we accepted the social safety net of food stamps, government cheese and peanut butter. But my Mother knew this wasn't a way of life, and she'd accept the hand up while finding better jobs.

So as I looked for work before school started, I found a job hanging insulation. I woke up in the dark of morning, working in heat with fiberglass and long sleeves, traveling in the back of a work van. But it was honest, hard work. Something my immigrant Mom taught me about. I worked with a great crew of guys, several Mexican, and one Irish bloke that introduced me to a shanty, half lager/

half lemonade. These guys helped inform my beliefs and understanding of immigrants. It didn't matter to me whether they were documented or not; I knew each of them as honest and hardworking, just like my immigrant Mother, they had a strong work ethic.

I continued dating Cheryl, the girl from High School, and made the three-hour drive from Goleta every couple of weeks to see her. Each week felt like it was getting more serious. I was convincing myself that marrying her would change everything about me to "normal."

## A Near-Death Experience

At some point in late 1985, shortly before my 19th birthday, I tired of the insulation work and the hours weren't going to be compatible while going to school. I borrowed my sister's mo-ped to go to a job interview in downtown Santa Barbara. I never arrived at the meeting.

I drove the mo-ped down one of the many one-way streets of Santa Barbara, into the downtown area, looked up at the cross-street to see where I was and slammed right into the back of a van stopped in front of a carpet store; I cracked the helmet I was wearing, which was the only thing that saved my life.

I woke up in the hospital, diagnosed with retrograde amnesia, needing a cane to walk, and had the epiphany that I was as I was meant to be. I didn't need to hide or avoid being gay. There was no judgment, and I was filled with such excitement that I could just be me, and I was OK with God.

I no longer believed those that told me I was a sinner, that I deserved to die. I no longer subscribed to the indoctrination of the prior 18 years. It was immediate, and I felt immediate peace with myself. I would have to break it off with Cheryl and hope I didn't break her heart in the process. I did love her, I just couldn't be authentic with her. And so it would be. I would finally admit to myself that which I'd been denying. But it was still not something I was ready to share with the whole family, or the world at that time.

I learned a few years later that Bob had witnessed the accident in which I was nearly killed. He worked at the carpet store at the time. In a city with a population of about 80,000, even assuming 10% are gay and half of those are men, what are the odds I'd wind up in a relationship with one who saw that? And that the shop owned by my sister's new father-in-law was on the same street? Staggering odds, which led me to believe we were meant to be connected.

After I'd recuperated, I took a job as a security guard at a facility associated with the Department of Defense. It allowed me to work shifts that didn't interfere with my class schedule. I went into college on the pre-med track. For many years before that, I only wanted to be a surgeon. I was carrying 16 quarter units, a full load, and working full-time to pay the bills, tuition and books. I became a connoisseur of various forms of tuna casserole. It was incredible what one box of mac and cheese, one can of tuna, one can of Veg-all and some breadcrumbs could create. I'd get two or three meals out of that.

So I worked and went to school. Money became tighter and tighter, and I wound up taking a second security guard job. This second job involved private security for some of the well-known stars and sports figures, and other well-to-do in Santa Barbara and Montecito. I recall on one property, I was driving up the driveway, my spotlight scanning the concrete structure that appeared to be built underground, save for the expansive window peeking out overlooking the Pacific Ocean. I was looking for anything unusual. I turned at the end of the driveway and headed back to the coded-entry gate when I saw a nude body rising from the hot tub as my searchlight passed over in that direction. The face was familiar, but I couldn't place this star's name in my mind. It wasn't until a few days later, while at a friend's house watching the Academy Awards, that I recognized her face—this time with clothes. "That's her!" I exclaimed. "That's the naked woman I saw coming out of the hot tub!"

Eventually, working two full-time jobs and carrying a full school load became too much for me to handle. I changed my major to English, hoping that would help, but I was utterly burned out. I knew I could no longer maintain the workload of juggling two full-time jobs and full school requirements. I dropped out after nearly two years. I needed a better paying job, so I applied to work at a local Credit Union. It was part-time, sorting mail and keeping up with office supplies, so I kept my star-studded security job and left the other.

## There's Something Happening Here

My sister married on March 20th, and I moved in with my roommates by April 1st, 1988. It was the first time I'd lived with anyone other than members of my immediate family. And in Santa Barbara, it was too expensive to not have a roommate, or in my case, two. Patty was the other roommate, and she was going to have a baby soon. Bob and I hung out together, introducing each other to our friends. After several months, Patty approached Bob. "Do you realize how much you two flirt with each other?" I was told she said. "Maybe there's something there between you."

As I was getting ready to go to bed on July 14th, at about 10:00pm, Bob approached me. "Do you have a few minutes to talk?" he asked.

"Sure." We went outside to the backyard, and sat beneath the stars on the wobbly picnic table he and a friend built.

"I was talking with Patty the other day," he started. "She thinks we flirt a lot with each other and as I thought about it, I think she's right. Is there something happening here? Is she right?"

There was definitely a spark taking place, something was happening, there was more "there" there than I had been willing to admit. I was falling for him, his wit, his charm, those eyes, and that smile and a sexy butt that even had my Mother commenting at one point. "Yeah, I think she is," I replied.

"So, where do we go from here?" he asked. I was in uncharted territory and never expected this.

"I don't know right now," I replied. "It's late, I need to work in the morning. Let's talk more tomorrow."

"OK," he said. I went to my room, he to his. I don't remember sleeping that night.

On the 16th, just two days later, we were helping a friend cater a party, taking trays of champagne through the guests. We were drinking along-side, and neither of us was sober by the time the party was over. We made it home and shared a bed for the first time. We decided that our anniversary would be July 15th, in between the understanding something more existed and the physical realization that something more was there. It was also the day my nephew was born.

Shortly after we got together, Patty moved out "annoyed with the new lovebirds," she joked. Since we were both still working poor, we needed a new roommate. As luck would have it, a friend of mine would be looking for a room, too.

I'd met Kaila at one of the Gay & Lesbian Resource Center events around sexuality and religion. It was a Bible study for those of us trying to reconcile the Faith we felt with the Faith we were told where our sexuality automatically made us sinners. I learned a lot during those study sessions, but the most important thing I learned was there was nothing wrong with the way I was made. I learned about ancient Aramaic and how the word "homosexual" didn't exist before the 1940s. I learned of multiple mistranslations, some honest, some specific. This is where I learned to distrust organized religion and to embark on a more 1-to-1 relationship with my Almighty.

Kaila easily fit right into the new household, even with her cat Gideon. The three of us went out to the bars or just hang out downtown or at the beach. We took road trips to San Francisco and Half Moon Bay. After coming out to a cacophony of Whitney Houston and similar pop music, I was introduced to the music of Melissa Etheridge by Kaila and her girlfriend. Melissa wasn't publicly out at the time, but it was a poorly kept secret among lesbians. One of my fondest memories was driving up the Pacific Coast Highway, with the four of us singing along to Melissa Etheridge. We were all glued to the TV when the Loma Prieta earthquake shook San Francisco with a magnitude of 6.9. We were worried about friends in the area before we had cell phones or social media.

Bob and I headed up the coast a few times a year to go camping in the Sequoias and to visit Big Sur. One of our favorite places was the Monterey Bay Aquarium, with its enormous circular tank in the middle. We usually wound up camping with friends of his that became my friends, too.

## The Dance We Shared

When I first introduced Bob to my family, we were still tentative on the whole relationship thing. I introduced him as my roommate to my sister, her husband, and my new nephew. When my Mother would visit the grandbaby, I also introduced her to Bob as my roommate. My Mother used to be a yard sale fanatic, and there was one event that took place annually in Santa Barbara that involved a neighborhood yard sale. Bob had a truck.

We took my Mom to many yard sale sites in the neighborhood. At one point, Bob saw a shovel for sale. "I need a shovel, but I don't have enough money."

"I do," I said. "I'll get it for you."

My Mother turned around and said, "You boys can just take it out in trade." Bob and I looked at each other and did everything we could not to laugh—or give away the secret, but for years to come, that would be a story that brought laughter to any room in which we told it. Eventually, even to my Mom.

My Mom. What can I say about her? She's always been there for me. She's been one person I know I could always depend upon. The person whose opinion I value most, and the one I try never to disappoint. As one might expect, coming out to her a few years prior was difficult for me. Not knowing what to expect after decades of hearing how evil we were, I was afraid. "Mom, I'm gay."

"Thank you for telling me," she calmly said. "That doesn't change the fact that I love you. I will love you no matter what." It was an undramatic coming out, but it was also clear she thought my sexuality was a phase, regardless of how many times I told her it wasn't. She was afraid I would die of AIDS, as she'd been told gay men do. She blamed herself because it must've been something she did to cause such a thing. She blamed my father, the divorce, and anything else trying to make sense of my being gay.

It was a surprise, then, after I'd shared that Bob and I were together, when she called him Son Number Two (after giving birth to two). She became a frequent guest in our homes over the years. Several times, in fact, she had gone to Santa Barbara to see doctors to perform neck and back surgeries on her, to help minimize the pain from degenerated discs, likely caused by the extreme physical activity of building homes. She would stay with us to recuperate since she still lived several hours away.

Likewise, Bob was welcomed entirely in her home. He joined me to visit or to go camping or horseback riding at the Ranch my parents were part owners of. Bob's mom died when he was young, growing up in Kenosha, Wisconsin. He once told me that before moving to California, he thought avocado was only a color one would get on kitchen appliances.

My Mom and Bob loved each other, and this relationship helped her understand that my sexuality was not a phase and that I could be happy living as a gay man. Similarly, my sister credits knowing Bob with opening her eyes and being less judgmental about homosexuality, especially after becoming a "born-again" Christian. "You're going to Hell and I'm worried about your soul," she'd told me when I came out to her. It strained our relationship for several years, but Bob made her feel at ease and realize that our relationship was just as natural as hers.

We were happy. In December 1989, we took a cruise to Mexico for my birthday when George H.W. Bush's administration nabbed Manuel Noriega. Traveling a few days on a ship from Long Beach to Ensenada, we were cramped in a tiny room. Still, the trip to Ensenada, via Catalina Island, was fantastic. Coming home, though, I was suffering from motion sickness while he was suffering from food poisoning. Once we were off the ship, we headed to my Mom's for Christmas at the Ranch. It was an extended family Christmas with my family and my step-father's family. Cousins, aunts, uncles, and parents gathered in at the cabin. This wound up being one of the best Christmas memories we would have, and one that is still talked about nearly 30 years later. It lacked all the pretentiousness of the holidays at home, where everything had to be perfectly decorated and adorned, the meal perfectly presented and timed. Instead, we focused on each other and the relaxed laughter.

We took many trips together over the years, mostly driving up the coast: Big Sur, Monterrey, and San Francisco. In the middle of the Russian River Valley, we found a Bed and Breakfast in Guerneville that catered to the gay community. We spent a few anniversaries there and went wine tasting. We got commemorative labels from the Korbel winery after President Clinton's inauguration. We even considered moving to the area.

Things were good. We'd been together a few years when I decided I wanted to adopt a puppy. I went to the shelter with the promise that I wasn't coming home with a dog unless they had a female German Shepard. And there she was: Soph. She was everything I wanted, and I named her after the Bette Midler character from her stand-up. She was a sweet dog with a beautiful disposition, and she would be with me for many years providing comfort on many tear-filled nights.

Bob had decided to go back to school as well, working on a landscape certification. Between both of our work and school schedules, we'd steal whatever time we could to visit friends, go to the bars, snuggle in front of the TV, or work in the yard in the garden. Sunday brunch at The Cajun Kitchen was a regular occurrence, especially after our server once informed us that the orange in a mimosa is "just for color." She knew how to pour! This was our "gay agenda," to live life every day and steal moments together that we could. Life was pretty consistent, which allowed me some flexibility to focus on my career and he on his.

I continued to advance at the Credit Union, eventually becoming the Accounting/Data Processing Manager. It was a lot of responsibility, long nights, and on-call work. I learned a lot about the systems we used to run the CU. I became adept at programming and simplifying the program used as well as writing macros that could make Lotus 1-2-3 sing. I gained the support and respect of the President of the CU. Still, eventually, I ran out of opportunities to either advance or be challenged in the job.

I left the Credit Union to start working for Santa Barbara Savings & Loan. In the late 1980s/early 1990s, we were in the midst of a financial meltdown of the S&L industry brought on by deregulation of the industry under the Reagan Administration. As it would happen, on one of our casual Fridays in April 1990, we were invaded by the blue suits from the RTC, the Resolution Trust Corporation. They kept us in the office for hours going over everything. I hadn't been working there long but wound up learning more than I expected as we went through the process of liquidating the thrift. I also returned to school in the evening attending the Community College studying Business Administration with an emphasis in Accounting. I was good at math and numbers, and it made sense to me.

The work environment was horrible, but I got a crash course in asset management and investor accounting practices. I became one of the few remaining in the Loan Accounting division, and I worked with the RTC in bundling and liquidating loan portfolios. It was months of agonizing work in a hostile environment with people of questionable moral integrity. I stayed for the opportunities to learn, and out of some feeling of pride in rapidly gaining responsibilities and increase in salary.

Eventually, the RTC did its job and liquidated all the assets and sold the failed Savings and Loan to Bank of America. My choice then was whether to remain working for BofA or find something else. I had loathed BofA since I was a customer and how they took advantage of customers. When I worked for the Credit Union, I moved away from Commercial Big Banks. This would wind up being significant in my career evolution, but it wasn't evident at the time.

I applied for work at a now-defunct Community Bank located in Oxnard, a 45+ minute drive south on the 101. They had recently acquired a loan portfolio that was being serviced in Orange County, and they were moving the operations to the headquarters. The entire Loan Servicing Department was being replaced by a new team in Oxnard. Given the experience I'd gained while being tortured by the RTC, I applied for a position doing Investor Accounting. The VP doing the hiring was a Latina woman about 10 years my senior, named Jessy Zamorano. We hit it off, she made an offer, and I declined. I would be commuting daily from Santa Barbara—a nearly 40-mile commute each direction, I'd told her. I simply couldn't afford the commute with gas and rental prices in Santa Barbara being what they were for what she offered. This, too, became a significant moment in my life.

Jessy eventually made me a counter-offer that I couldn't turn down, and I was suddenly commuting on Highway 101 to work every day. I remember the first day, we were still moving into the office. Boxes were everywhere and remained for several months while waiting on a filing system to be installed. On that first day, I met Julie, one of my colleagues in the Loan Servicing Department. My first impression was that her cheery disposition and my personality were going to clash. Thank goodness I was wrong because she became one of my closest friends. I can recall going through the boxes of files while the radio broadcast the Clarence Thomas confirmation hearings. I also remember the person hired to be the manager disappearing for hours at end and returning reeking of cologne.

I had, once again, found myself in a hostile work environment. This time, it wasn't an overly aggressive regulator sexually harassing me. It also wasn't the same overly aggressive regulator verbally harassing me, but it was a hostile environment, nonetheless. Julie and I discussed what was happening. Jessy had realized she'd hired an incompetent monster, and he was gone within 6 months of hire. "I wanted to hire you for the manager job," she'd told me years later. "That was my biggest mistake, getting talked into hiring him." It was time for another change in my trajectory as I was promoted to interim, then permanent, Loan Servicing Manager.

Eventually, the hours' long commute took a toll, and the opportunity arrived for us to move somewhere it was a little more affordable and closer to the office in Ventura. We packed up the house and the dogs and rented a house in Ventura, moving on July 4th weekend, 1993. The added responsibility resulted in longer hours, more headaches, and an increased salary. Since Bob had been working in landscaping and studying landscape design, he took the opportunity to study further and work for a local nursery.

I dug in and transformed the department. I re-engineered processes, modified our accounting system, and developed a written policies and procedures manual. We'd turned a loss center into a profit center within a year. The income per loan was up nearly 17%, while expenses per loan were down 33%. It was a phenomenal turnaround, and I was the only department head that wasn't at least an AVP in my Title. But I got the attention of management. This is a cautionary tale to be careful of what you ask for. The notice was around how they could take the gains I facilitated and sell off the assets. I worked myself, and my team, out of jobs.

I spent the next several months with the heads of HR, Finance, and the Lending Departments negotiating severance packages and incentives for my team. I was expected to remain at the Bank in another capacity. It's here I learned the critical lesson of documentation and covering your own ass. It was also through this experience that I received a severance that, combined with our savings, allowed us to buy a home.

That May, I accepted a job as the Loan Servicing Manager at a local Credit Union. I quickly found the need to reorganize and restructure the department processes and worked with our teams to increase the efficiencies. It was challenging, I was appreciated for my efforts, and I felt I'd found a home where I could prosper.

On July 4th, 1994, Bob and I bought our first house. We put in a down payment on a brand-new construction. Our first home was a slab of concrete. In the process of doing so, our names are memorialized on the Ventura Pier.

We watched as the walls went up, as the roof went on, as the carpet and cabinets were installed. When we closed escrow on October 17th, we were the proud owners of a three-bedroom, cookie-cutter home on the east side of Ventura. We had a barren backyard, save for the little slab outside the sliding door, but at least the front yard was landscaped.

It was an odd-shaped lot, one we chose specifically for the size of the land, though we had an easement across the back and right side of the property, limiting what we could do or plant. But it allowed Bob to design and install a landscape that would be a showcase for his skills. He was like a painter with a blank canvas ready to prepare his masterpiece.

But it was slow-going heading into the fall and winter months, and even in Southern California, we still had holidays and weather to deal with sometimes. And after scraping everything we had to close escrow, money was tight. Just two weeks later, our neighborhood was inundated with kids bussed in for Halloween. It was a new neighborhood, and we were in Phase 2 of 5 for the development. Many of us in Phase 2 moved in at the same time, including our next-door-neighbors.

He loved Christmas. I should have known when I saw the half-tree tacked to the wall in the living room of that Santa Barbara bungalow on that March day when I interviewed to move in as a roommate. We would help a shop-owner friend of his decorate the store for Christmas, stringing garland, lights, and ornaments around the store. The friend was only happy when he was miserable. But that never mattered to Bob. He lived for the lights and the decorations, and he decorated our house that first year. My family came to visit and share Christmas with us that year. We probably went overboard with the gift-giving, but we'd met a significant goal in being adults and were dreaming of a long, bright future together.

## Diagnosis

I've heard that if you want to make God laugh, tell Him your plans. Sweet Scout, the Golden Retriever, was diagnosed with cancer shortly after we moved into the first house we bought together. Then, in February 1995, Bob noticed a lump on his inner thigh. This was God beginning to chuckle, which I believe turned into a full-on belly laugh within a matter of months.

The diagnosis came on the fourth anniversary of his father's death, March 15th, after a biopsy that he was suffering from non-Hodgkins lymphoma. We also learned this was brought on by a compromised immune system. He was HIV-positive, technically suffering from AIDS. Having the diagnosis made our heads spin. In the nearly seven years we were together, this was unexpected, but then again, not really. We always used condoms, never knowing for sure the status of the other person. It never dawned on us to get tested. We were still both healthy, recovering quickly from anything that ever knocked us down. There was no way either of us had a compromised immune system, so there was obviously an error in the test results for him.

We retested him and tested me. The next two weeks or so were hell as we waited for the results of the tests. He was beside himself, thinking he'd killed me. "I'm so sorry," he wept. "I don't want to be the one to kill you."

"You won't," I reassured him, hoping I was right. "Let's get you better."

We'd lost friends over the years to this disease, but we'd also seen friends get treated and be pulled back from death's door.

The results were returned. Bob's diagnosis didn't change. He was HIV-positive, I was not. After seven intimate years together, in a monogamous relationship, we proved the efficacy of condoms in preventing the spread of HIV. Now we knew what we were dealing with, and we knew how people would react to the "AIDS" word. For now, he was suffering from cancer.

He began chemotherapy in March. Everything we'd ever seen or heard about chemotherapy was right. He was sicker, run-down, being poisoned. On April 23rd, Scout had had enough, and we took him to the vet to let him go. The parallels felt prescient to us, and we cried with a depth of sorrow neither of us had experienced before. He was afraid of his family's reaction should they know he was HIV+. This was the only time I'd ever met any of his extended family aside from his brother. They were helpful.

We kept the underlying diagnosis to ourselves and the medical staff. Still, as Bob got sicker and needed hospitalization, the tag on the door for additional precautions was making it difficult to keep it under wraps. That's how my Mom found out; she'd asked one of the nurses why the extra precautions and she was upset in thinking that we'd put her in danger. This was the time in which we lived, ruled more by fear by those that didn't know just how difficult it was to be infected by HIV. She was assured by the medical staff that she wasn't in any danger as long as she followed the protocols. Our lack of disclosure caused a rift of anger and distrust.

"You should have told me!" she said. "You put my life in danger!" She was angry, beside herself.

"I would never put you in danger," I tried to reassure her. "As long as you took the precautions, you were never in any danger. I've lived with him for 7 years, and I'm fine," I reminded her, hoping to again reassure her safety. "I'm sorry, we didn't think anyone needed to know."

I'd spent years hiding the truth, trying to "protect his reputation," as if being exposed to a disease and dying from it would impact his reputation. Though, in those days, it did. They made HIV/AIDS an issue of morality, or the lack thereof. It was sinful behavior that led to the disease transmission.

So it would be, throughout the 1980's and well into the 1990's that only "they" got this disease. I remember watching an episode of The Golden Girls where this topic was addressed: Rose had received a blood transfusion, she was rightfully scared (in those days, a positive diagnosis meant you were very likely going to die), the other girls tried to calm her down, and she lashed out at promiscuous Blanche—as if her sexuality were reason enough for her to be exposed since Rose was "a good girl."

And when asked why Bob was in the hospital, or later how he died, my response was always the same: "He had non-Hodgkins lymphoma, he died of cancer." It wasn't anyone's business that it was because of his compromised immune system. He became another statistic.

During Bob's treatment, there were several instances of hospitalization needed. The nurses at the hospital were incredible people that didn't care that we were two men together. "Back again, are we?" I recall once.

"We can't get enough of the 5-star accommodations and cuisine," he'd joke.

And the nurses loved him. I spent too many days and nights in that hospital; they brought in a cot for me to sleep on. We watched worn out VCR tapes on the one TV/VCR they had on a rolling cart. After Bob died, I donated a new TV/VCR combination and cart in his memory. We were able to spend much needed time together to talk, to cry, to share our truths and bond at such an intimate level that there were no barriers.

When not in the hospital, he'd be at home researching and designing the backyard. Early on in the treatment, he'd feel well enough to dig and plant some while I was working at the Credit Union. He continued working part-time until he couldn't any longer. And then we spent time talking about our lives and our memories.

There was one time, after a particularly brutal round of chemotherapy, that we sat on the sofa in the living room. I was holding him while he was crying. "I just can't find the joy in life anymore," he cried. He wanted to give up, and I couldn't blame him. I hated seeing him suffer like this. Before I could say anything, a yellow, tropical-looking bird landed in one of the King Palms he'd planted in the back yard, its movements catching our eyes. He watched the bird for a few moments, started crying again, and said, "I've found some joy."

## Didn't Anyone Tell You?

"Didn't anyone tell you?" he asked. "It's terminal."

That's how this doctor we had never met before broke the news; there was nothing more to do for him. That bedside manner infuriated me for years. "Didn't anyone tell you?"

We spent the Fourth of July 1995 with my parents. I was helping my step-father Jim paint around the house, and Bob was enjoying the mountain air and views. Jim started experiencing stomach pains that weekend. It would be the last time Bob would visit my parents' home or see that mountain range. We'd had some good memories together in the Kern River Valley, but we had to cut this visit short because he wasn't feeling well.

We wound up in the hospital a few days later, the last time we'd be sleeping there. "Didn't anyone tell you?"

I arranged for hospice care to take care of him at home. Neither of us wanted him to die in a hospital. I moved furniture so we could have a hospital bed and a daybed next to him for me downstairs. We moved him home on July 27th. Father David, a Catholic priest friend of Bob's, visited that day and married us in God's eyes. It was a small, intimate gathering.

We'd scheduled the back patio to be poured before this news. Bob had designed a landscape with rounded, undulating patterns in both the plantings and concrete patio while I'd designed the patio cover and dug the holes for the footings. We were able to wheel him out into the backyard so he could start seeing it come together.

My Mom came to help take care of him while I was needing to work during the day. I took over at night. As he lay on the bed where he would die, we had the most intimate of conversations. We wrote his obituary, we spoke of pain and pleasure in our relationship, and we forgave each other for any slights or distress caused. After seven years, our life wasn't always perfect. Daily stress in bills, work, an unexpected injury, and pain took their toll on us, but we did our best for each other.

For a moment, without the toxic chemo coursing through his veins, he gained strength. That prayer for a miracle would either remain unanswered, or I had been told, "No."

The cycle repeated for three weeks until August 10th, when I stayed home from work. We knew the time we had was limited.

> *Robert John Roders*
> *September 9, 1959–August 14, 1995*

## Grief and Recovery
### Grieving—The First Year (or so)

What does a 28-year-old with a seven-year relationship know about being a widower? What could I possibly know about grieving and how to grieve and how to deal with my life being shattered? "We" were no longer "us;" "our" dreams died with him, and frankly, so did "I." "I" was no longer the "me" I was as part of "we." Though I remained an individual person, "I" was defined, in part, by my relationship with him. "I" was his partner, his caretaker, his lover. "I" was part of "we," where "we" made plans, "we" celebrated, "we" cleaned the house and "we" went grocery shopping.

And so, I would have to find my way through the grief, learning lessons along the way. I'd stumble, I'd do things that were perfectly normal to me in my mind, but in hindsight were incredibly destructive. And I didn't care. I was a widowed 28-year-old that lost the love of my life. It wasn't just that I didn't care. I didn't give a single fuck about anything, and, if it weren't for my Mother being alive, I would have seriously considered ending my life in those early months. And I did think about it. I just knew I couldn't do that to my Mom.

Instead of downing a handful of pills or slicing my wrists open, I opted for the extended version of suicide: I drank. A lot. I smoked. A lot. I ate all the wrong foods, didn't sleep unless I'd passed out drunk. I would work during the day, and each night I'd come home to the dog and an empty house. I'd get to work in the back yard on the planting, irrigation, or building the patio cover I'd designed.

Many times while wallowing in my numbness, I'd notice a hummingbird in the yard. They're not uncommon where we lived in Ventura, and the males do tend to be territorial. Still, there was one that always made an appearance whenever I thought of Bob or mentioned him aloud.

The numbness. I remember that sensation well. It allowed me to push friends away, the ones that reminded me of him and "us." We had other coupled friends that would reach out, but I couldn't deal with other couples being happy. I'd decline with one excuse or another before they'd eventually stop calling altogether. It allowed me to throw the fucks I had out the window, and I found myself drinking more to numb myself more. I went to precisely three places: Work, grocery store, and Grief Group.

I'm an introvert. Sharing comes with difficulty to me, but once I'm comfortable with someone, and I've built that rapport, I can be a loyal friend and confidant. Less than four months after Bob died, Jessy called me. She had become a good friend, one of the few that wouldn't allow me to make excuses. Her significant other, Dodge, had just been killed in an accident in Mexico. We spent many hours on the phone many times trying to make sense of it all.

I vividly recall the first night I'd gone to the Grief Support Group. I was numb, probably buzzed. I heard a woman welcome me, "It gets better," she said. I wanted to curse this little old lady out. How could she possibly know that? It dawned on me, finally; she's lived past this part. She's a widow. It was an eclectic Group, some with spouses gone a few years, some a few days; some elderly, some in their 50's, and me in my 20's; some Jewish, some not. Everyone but me was straight.

And it didn't matter to them. They could tell in my grief-filled eyes the depth of my love for Bob and the pain I was in and for the first time since I don't know when, I felt accepted for just being who I was, and who I was, at that time, was a grieving husband. This Group would become part of my chosen, extended family. We supported each other through triumphs, such as Chris finding a new love and getting remarried; we supported each other through the lows, such as friends or family dying. We went out to eat frequently outside of Group to simply socialize and not have to explain what being a widower was like. And this Group, led by Roni Peterson, would be instrumental in helping me lift myself up to move on.

But that would take time and a whole lot of work on my part. It wasn't going to be one thing that made it all better, that made me look towards living my life again, but it would take many forms of action. Some good, some not so good. Some I freely share and recommend to other widows and widowers I encounter, and some I suggest those same people avoid. Some I read about or learned about in Group and others I discovered by myself.

One of the first things I discovered was that the calendar before August 14, 1995, did not exist. This was Day Zero for me. The "EVENT." I would measure all sense of time against this date. Yes, things happened before then. However, the frame of reference was from the date he died. I measured progress first in days, then weeks, then months. Eventually, my frame of reference was in years. In a way, his death date became my new birthday because I was no longer "me" (that part of "we"), I was becoming "me," an individual.

Another thing I learned is that this new timeline of Day Zero is not experienced the same universally. The friends I'd managed not to alienate didn't use the same point of reference, except in cases where they were remarking specifically about Bob's death. And those that barely knew either of us or even some that we worked with, would think, "it's been x-number of months, Jim should be over it by now." That's honestly one of the most frustrating and disrespectful things I'd ever heard while mourning. As if there's a required time to mourn and express grief.

Here's the truth: no timeline works for everyone. Anyone who grieves will do so at their own pace. There is no wrong answer. I have a friend that started dating six weeks after his wife passed. "How disrespectful!" I heard from people unfamiliar with this couple and what they went through together. My friend's journey is his to experience. For myself, it was several years before I'd allow myself to be vulnerable enough to let someone in. It doesn't mean I loved

Bob more than my friend loved his wife; it merely shows that we all grieve as individuals.

It was easier for me to withdraw from the majority of social activities. And I wrote and listened to music and found feelings and expressed emotions via a journal, writing, or music. Creating "something" was therapeutic to me.

After a while, I got tired of people asking me how I was doing. "Do you really want to know, or are you just being polite?" I'd ask. Very rarely did anyone really want to know what I was feeling at that particular moment. But those souls brave enough to ask got the truth. In most cases, the response I received was, "I can guess," or "No, not really."

There was one co-worker who said, "Of course I do!" I told her, "I hate my life. I hate living like this. I wish I could have him back and I hate crying all the time." This queued the tears and she simply hugged me saying, "It's OK. It's understandable."

I found journaling to be incredibly cathartic. There was something about putting pen to paper and getting all those emotions and thoughts out. I wrote Bob letters, like this one early on.

> *09/07/95*
> *Dear Bob,*
> *Thought I'd try writing you a letter—*
> *therapy with a pen.*

*First of all, I wanted to tell you how much I love you and miss you. It's been nearly three weeks since at least 72 of your loved ones gathered to say "goodbye." Ed & Henriette Setterfield were among those 72. As you know, Ed passed away last week and today is his birthday.*

*I went to his services yesterday and cried not only tears for him, but tears for you as well – especially when Henriette's sister told Ed that he and Andrew were going to work in the gardens of heaven. That's what we told you. I hope that you are all working together—at least you won't have to work on the roses!*

*I hope you're happy up there. I hope everything we told you is true.*

*I know you tried to come back the other night. I think to say goodbye. I wasn't ready and I pretty much refused to let you. I know that wasn't fair to either of us, but I just wasn't ready. I don't know when I'll be ready, but you may visit any time—just to talk. And I hope you will be able to visit many more times and, when I'm ready, I'll let you say "goodbye." I want you to be clear on this issue, I didn't reject you because I don't love you or miss you. It's precisely because of how much I love and miss you.*

*I can't seem to forget about you for any period of time. As the Pet Shop Boys would say, "You are always on my mind." I'm trying to keep busy, but it's not so easy. I want to, but I'm having a hard time getting motivated. I just feel so empty inside.*

*I have a hard time believing that you're gone. I was there, I've seen your ashes, I know, intellectually, that you're gone, but I still expect to see you. I guess that's normal.*

*I wanted to thank you for our seven years together. Sure, we had our problems but, in hindsight, they paled in comparison, until you got sick, but we still managed a few good times. I also wanted to thank you for squeezing my hand when you left. I think it was your way of saying that it was OK.*

*After all, Mom and I kept telling you that it was OK. I wonder if that was the right thing to say. I'm sorry I gave you permission to go, but I also didn't want to see you suffer any more. I miss you.*

*I regret that I only let you see the strong me, not the scared me. The scared me snuck through a few times, but I hope you know that I was not unaffected by your illness. I thought I had to be strong to give you strength to keep fighting. I realize*

*now, a little too late, that you already had*
*the strength.*
   *I love you. J.*

   I would explore how I felt grocery shopping for one
(I didn't like it). There was no topic I didn't address at
one point or another in the years I wrote following The
Event. I would later type all those hand-written entries
and add commentary that came from the passage of
time and wisdom of afterthought being a widower that
"survived." As I read those words now, I recognize that
back then, my interpretation lacked a maturity that,
frankly, only more time and the perspective of age would
provide. I was only 30 or so when I started writing, and
really hadn't lived a lot. Nor did I have the benefit of
reflective time.

   My journal book (with commentary) would span
250 pages and three years of recovery. If one were to read
it now, they'd see I hit every point of the Kubler-Ross
model of grief: denial, anger, bargaining, depression, and
acceptance. One thing to know about this model is that the
"progression" through these steps is non-linear, nor are they
necessarily logical or even a "progression," for that matter.
Logically, I knew Bob was dead, but I still tried to bargain
with God for one more day. "I'd give anything to have you
here with me again," I wrote. "I'm so fucking angry at you
for leaving me!" I also wrote. Sometimes, I'd write those
sentiments in the same entry.

What I have learned: Grieving isn't logical. Here's another thing I learned about grieving: nobody can tell you how to do it. And you shouldn't listen to anyone telling you how to grieve, and for the love of everything, don't compare your journey with any other's journey! Just because my friend started dating 6 weeks later, doesn't mean I needed to. It was two years before I threw away Bob's toothbrush.

It's perfectly normal to be angry at the person who left you, as it was for me. It's perfectly normal to be angry at whatever Deity you worship (if any) for taking your loved one away from you. I learned that my life was ripped apart and shred all over the place, and I had a right to be angry. We only had seven years and were planning for the future, someday.

"Someday" never came. Damned right, I was angry. And even after finding a new life, it still angers me and I still wonder, despite what I found later, "what if...?" What would our lives be like after 30 years together? Would we have stayed together all that time?

Those questions can never be answered, which adds to the anger. Focusing on the unanswerable types of questions led me to a level of depression I'd never experienced. What I was going through was situational depression, which is understandable. How I decided to work through that depression wasn't. As I mentioned, I drank a lot and filled my days and nights working and drinking. I didn't mix drinking at work, but it could have been easy enough for me to fall into that. When I realized the wine didn't have the desired effect anymore, I switched to bourbon. I didn't want to feel, and passing out would put me in that space. I eventually started paying attention to what I was doing to myself. I worked on honoring Bob's memory by trying to enjoy life as he did, and as I had promised him I would. It's a good thing I was never seduced by drugs. If I were, I could easily see myself using them to escape what was causing me such pain.

Instead, I began feeling comfort and acceptance with my new found Group of fellow widows and widowers. Roni was a fantastic facilitator of discussion and allowing us to experience and share what we were going through.

We explored themes of grief, which included guilt - survivor's guilt, specifically. It appeared to me, through anecdotal evidence in our Group, to be part of the process. No matter what anyone says, you can't help but feel guilty about something. I felt guilty about what I did before he got sick. I felt guilty about not being more sensitive when the lump appeared, as if by my sensitivity, he would still be alive. If I had only known then what I know now, I would have taken him to the doctor immediately. As if that would have saved his life. Eventually, I began to realize that no matter what I did or, just as importantly, what I didn't do, the outcome could not have changed. For my own sanity, I had to fall back to the faith-teachings of my youth. I had to believe that there is a higher power and a purpose for everything that happens. I had to believe that we are allotted a specific amount of time on this earth and, no matter what, when it's our time, it's our time. I had to believe that "God works in mysterious ways" and that it wasn't up to me to question the Almighty. I had to believe these things or I would still feel guilty. And I also realized that, no matter what happened, it was out of my hands. I couldn't save Bob from what was happening, no matter how much I wanted or how much I tried.

I felt guilty because I was still here; I got the house and a small life insurance settlement. And, more importantly, I got to live and continue to experience. And somehow, that didn't seem fair. Especially since I felt so empty. Nothing I did could fill the void. The drinking didn't help. Work didn't fill me. Finishing the house and spending money on things I didn't really need couldn't fill the emptiness. In the irrationality of grieving, I even equated being numb with that being a feeling.

If I were going to get past this point, I knew I had to do the work. As I mentioned, we did many different exercises. One that struck me the hardest was when we discussed dialoguing with our loved one. I read later that this technique should really be done under the guidance of a counselor. Still, it was one of the most incredible experiences in my life to experience. I wrote a dialogue between Bob and me, just about six weeks after he'd died, but it resonated so much to me. I started consciously, and at some point in the exchange, it became automatic.

*09/25/95–from my journal*

*J: Hi, honey.*

*B: Hey, you.*

*J: Just thought I'd say "hi" and let you know how much I miss you.*

*B: I know, I miss you too.*

*J: You've been gone six weeks, and sometimes the pain is so much that I can hardly function.*

*B: I know. I've been watching you. It's OK, really. I'm not in pain and I'm with people I love—Mom and Dad, John and Chuck. John and I paid you a visit the other day. It was good to hear you laugh and see you smile again.*

*J: I have a hard time smiling, but your visit with John made me laugh. I miss you both.*

*B: But it's OK to smile and laugh.*

*J: But I need to cry. I miss you so much. I'm having a really hard time with this. I know you know how much I love you.*

*B: I do. I loved you, too. I didn't want to leave you, but I had to.*

*J: I know. It doesn't make it any easier, though. I thought I was tough and strong. Guess I'm not.*

*B: Yes, you are. You gave me strength when I really needed it. Now, I need to repay the favor.*

*J: Like the other day?*

*B: Yes, you needed to know that I was there for you—always. "I promise you tomorrow, the sun is gonna shine."*

*J: I know the sun will shine, but you won't be there.*

*B: I'm always there. I'm part of you.*

*J: Yes, you are. You always will be. I don't know if I'll ever live without you.*

*B: Yes, you will. I'll always be there to make sure you're OK.*

*J: I hope so. I'll always need you.*

Tears covered my face and the spell was interrupted by a phone call. It was Bob's brother. He asked if I had a cold. "No," I told him, "I'm crying." We talked for about an hour or so before hanging up. I tried to resume the connection to Bob, but I fell short of the trance-like writing.

*B: So, my brother called. I appreciate your being there for him.*

*J: I'm there for you.*

*B: And I appreciate it. And I love you for it.*

*J: I love you, too. I miss you so much, it's hard to describe.*

*B: It's OK, I know. Remember that I love you, that I will always love you no matter what.*

*J: And I will always love you. You are my life.*

*B: Life is more than that.*

*J: No, it's not. You are my life, you are part of me. I can't let that go.*

*B: You don't need to. Make me part of you.*

*J: You already are. I'm tired, dear, I need to go to bed.*

*B: OK. We'll talk later. I love you and I'll visit as soon as I can.*

*J: I'd like that. I love you so much. I miss you more than I can say.*

*B: Me, too. Goodnight, Pookie.*

*J: Goodnight, Love.*

As I read what I'd written, I didn't remember writing most of it. I do believe there was a paranormal, psychic connection in that conversation. I was so sure of the connection that I tried again the next day, again to fail. I wrote, instead, words I thought I needed to hear coming from him. I needed to hear them, but they weren't real.

Bob and I shared a love of music, and at this time we mostly listened to country music with some pop thrown in for good measure. There were many times I'd think of him or of a song, like *The Dance,* and then I would hear it on the radio or TV moments later. When it happens frequently, it's hard to chalk it up to coincidence. I believe "there are more things in Heaven and Earth than are dreamt of in your philosophy," to borrow from the Bard. I think "The Universe" gives us signs and gives us what we need, whether a song on the radio or, in one instance, a substitute grief counselor during Group one night. I recall not really wanting to go that night, but I decided to go anyway.

Roni was sick and it was a small Group of five of us that night. Debbie was our substitute counselor, and I found out she also worked with Bob while he was dying. "You were the love of his life," she told me nearly four months after he died. "He told me he appreciated all you did for him." Of course, this brought tears to my eyes to have my thoughts validated that he did love and appreciate me. "He was very concerned about you, about how you are going to be, and that you shouldn't be alone. I believe you two were soulmates."

It was signs like this that helped me from day-to-day, because I knew he wasn't *really* gone—he'd simply taken his thread around the corner as Gillian said.

The loneliness was overwhelming. Imagine spending a quarter of your life, nee 70% of your adult life, with someone, wholly and fully integrated into your life, day in and day out, and suddenly having them... gone. While it may have only been seven years, in context it was a significant part of my existence until then. Daytime, with the distractions of work and other people, was more tolerable. Nighttime was the worst, though. Aside from Soph, I was alone with my thoughts in a quiet home. I didn't have work to distract me and TV could only do so much. When I wasn't working in the yard or drinking or going to grief counseling or writing, I was thinking of ways in which I could channel my thoughts and process my grief, not only for myself but to express in such a way as to share with others what it FELT like to be going through this.

I mentioned a love for music, and for this introvert, the emotions music can illicit was a great way to share my thoughts and feelings. It would take over a year, but I wound up compiling 69 songs to share on three cassette tapes. I designed the artwork, wrote the liner notes explaining why each song was chosen and put great care in the creation of the playlist order of the songs. I would queue the source track and record it to tape. In February 1996, I released the first compilation. This was the "Grief is Killing Me" tape, with songs that questioned why and a longing for the past. In June, I released the second compilation. This became known as the "Attitude" tape. This was my expression of the anger and the longing I felt. February 1997 brought Volume III, the "Hopeful" tape.

I created the first tape in advance of taking Bob's ashes and spreading them as he'd wished. I had a necklace made that I could carry some of his ashes in; it wasn't commercial back then, so it was a custom silver vial I hung around my neck. On April 1, 1996, my family joined me on a hike. Jim, Karen, Mom and I drove up to the Johnsondale Bridge, along the upper Kern River. We hiked about 45 minutes until I found a spot overlooking the river, a California Oak providing shade from the direct sun, a slight cove providing some shelter from the worn footpath. I'd mixed his ashes with some wildflower seeds. I cleared the ground cover, and dug a shallow swath in the moist earth. I spread out the ashes mixed with seeds, and gently covered them with soil and mulch, tears falling down my cheeks.

> *"To every thing there is a season, and a time to every purpose under the heaven;*
> *A time to be born, and a time to die; a time to plant, and a time to pluck up that which is planted;*
> *A time to kill, and a time to heal; a time to break down, and a time to build up;*
> *A time to weep, and a time to laugh; a time to mourn, and a time to dance;*
> *A time to cast away stones, and a time to gather stones together; a time to embrace, and a time to refrain from embracing;*
> *A time to get, and a time to lose; a time to keep, and a time to cast away;*

*A time to rend, and a time to sew; a time
to keep silence, and a time to speak;*
*A time to love, and a time to hate; a time
of war, and a time of peace."*

We read from Ecclesiastes 3. Karen shared a letter she'd
written before Bob died:

*"Dearest Bob,*
*We will never forget your smile or
your personality. We will never forget your
green thumb.*
*As you grew things here on earth, I pray
your spirit grows even more in heaven.*
*I know you are going to a better
place where there is a different kind of
human race.*
*We'll all be together someday when that
cloud comes to take us away*
*You don't have to wait any longer for that
date of fate... God has called you close to Him,
He's taking you away from Jim and all of your
loved ones.*
*But don't worry for us, 'cause we'll be
okay, we'll just be waiting for our glorious day
when we meet again in the sky so high.*
*'Til then, your memory will never die. We
love you forever, Bob."*

I returned to this spot on the first Anniversary of Bob's death, August 14, 1996. I had such plans! I wrote him a letter. I tied it to a balloon, releasing some of the emotions and constraints that held onto me. I planned to set the balloon free at the precise moment one year later that he took his last breath. Instead, here's my journal entry about the day:

> *"Well, the hour has passed, and I survived. Of course, nothing went as planned. Halfway through the hike, the balloon popped. I got to the spot early, and there were no flowers. Disappointed, I listened to some music, turned around, and headed back to Mom's house. I stopped off to get a balloon, but they didn't have much in the way of selection. So, I picked up a few, tied the note to them, and set them free. They didn't even clear the treetops. Snagged in the pine tree and popped. My letter to Bob was dangling precariously in a tree in my mother's yard. A fucked up day."*

This day wound up being a comedy of errors and I could almost hear God laughing at me again, but it was frustrating and heartbreaking when it happened. The intent was to hike to the spot, by myself, listen to some music I'd brought for a memorial, and then release the balloon. It was a very simple plan.

And I was heartbroken when the balloon popped
the first time on the hike. I really wanted to be there, at
that exact hour of his last breath, with the balloon ready
to go. I didn't have the time (based on my self-imposed
schedule) to go back and get another balloon and, it
being in a rural area, it's not like it was at the corner
store. I nearly broke down and cried on the spot, but I
just said, "fuck it" and continued up the mountain. I was
determined, so I walked quickly. So quickly, that I found
the spot nearly 30 minutes earlier than I had expected.
But no flowers were blooming. It was dry and hot, and
the wildflower seeds didn't seem to take or they were
seasonal and gone. Again, I was heartbroken and just
about to cry. I listened to some music, and figured, "You
know what? This isn't working for me." So I got all my
stuff together, said goodbye to Bob's ashes, and walked
back to the car.

I decided to get another balloon, and when I say there
wasn't much selection, I mean to say there was one choice –
pearl white. And there were only two choices in ribbon:
white and hot pink. Instead of one balloon, I decided I'd
use two, tied with the hot pink ribbon. I tied the note to the
ribbons attaching the balloons. I found a spot in the yard
of my parents' house that looked pretty open and set the
balloons and my letter to Bob free. The wind picked up and
threw the balloons into the pine tree, popping the balloons
and there, dangling from the hot pink ribbon, was my letter
to Bob. Again, I almost cried.

But, I was determined, and I really wanted to get that letter up to him. The only problem was, I couldn't reach it, so I had to write another note to him. And, when I went to get dinner that evening, I went to get another balloon. I found a clearer spot in the yard with fewer trees, and was just about to let the balloon and note go when the wind shifted directions – it would have put the balloon in the same tree! So I moved again, and the balloon made it over the trees and continued its heavenward climb. The original letter, meanwhile, still dangled in the trees.

I'm not sure when it did, but tree released this original letter from its grasp and I found it on the ground.

*"August 14, 1996*

*Dearest Pookie,*

*I can't believe you've been gone from me for a year already. It seems like only yesterday that we were together.*

*I'm having a hard time saying goodbye to you—I just can't seem to get over the years we spent together . I know I'll never fully get beyond your death and the impact it has had on me.*

*Part of me hopes that as I take this hike through the mountains to where we laid your ashes, that I fall from the cliff and die. Yet, I know that it isn't' my time to see you yet. Though how I wish I could. My dreams just* aren't enough to sustain me anymore. I'd much rather be in your arms again.

I remember many things about our years together—the good, the bad, and even the ugly. Your last impression in my mind is haunting. I still see your face and body as it was when you died. I know that wasn't really you, just a shell, but it hurts no less.

I'm continuing on just surviving being without you. Your love was all I needed, and all you gave. I miss many things about your physical presence—your smile, your laugh, your eyes, your mischievous grin, your very existence in this world. I know we had our problems, but those we worked on. And the important thing was that we were always there for each other when it mattered most. And, when it comes right down to it, that's all that mattered, really.

I love you now as much as I ever did. I know I need to move on, but it's so damned hard to do it. Even though you're gone, I still worry about you and I feel you worry about me. Our love knows no boundaries, and even death can't stop it. See you soon.

*All my love, J"*

## Grief Group 2–Advanced Healing

It had been 18 months by the time I got to the "Hopeful" tape.

There had been a lot more writing and self-inspection going on during this time, which is why the third, and last volume of music, had a more hopeful tone for the future because the work we did in Group was focused on us, and our future, not on the loss.

Some of us had "graduated" from Grief Group 1 and were working on more intense practices in the healing process.

The first year was all about the firsts. I see no possibility that I would have been able to tackle the work from Grief Group 2 any earlier. In each session, we were given some homework to do. We came together to share what we'd written, comment on, and encourage, each other's growth. I thank the stars for the facilitator we had. She had the foresight and suggestion to break the Group up. Newbies, like I was that first Group night hearing "It'll get better" from someone I didn't know, have a different focus. When those of us who have already experienced the newness of loss are exposed to a newbie, it tends to drag us back to that place where we initially suffered the death. We weren't progressing in our healing as new members arrived. And still, 25 years later, when I meet a new widow or widower, I'm brought back to that first meeting and the rawness of the pain. But also, with decades of experience under my belt now, I also try to offer hope in a future of life after loss.

Roni was again our facilitator. Having worked with most of us for a year or more, her focus was for us to do the hard work needed to move forward. I wouldn't suggest anyone try without a trained counselor, and our Grief Group 2 explored themes such as:

- When we speak about our loved one, we often say something like, "a piece of me died with him." Identify and write about that piece of you that died.

- How do you comfort or take care of yourself?

- What have you done to make new friends and bring new people into your life?

- Seeds of a new self are growing. What seeds are you planting?

- Finish these statements: I'm beginning to notice... and I'm aware of...

- What are the things you like most about yourself? And the things you would like to change about yourself?

- What would happen if you let go of the pain?

- What strengths have you gained as a result of the loss?

- What do you still need help with for your grieving?

- What three things are you grateful for?

• Write about what it means to be free to you.

Some of these themes took several weeks to get through. It was difficult because they each forced me to look inward for solutions, to understand that I alone have the power to determine how I react and also challenge myself to look to a future. My future had died with Bob. I had nothing to look forward to, so this work was the heavy lifting.

Shortly before the two-year mark, I had an unsettling dream of Bob. It wasn't the first disturbing dream, and I feel fortunate I was able to dream of him frequently. Except, this dream really felt different. The details were fuzzy when I wrote about it, but I remembered I could literally feel him kiss me, but it felt like he was kissing me specifically to tell me good-bye. While that was upsetting, I was also at a point in my life where I thought I was doing better. I thought I was ready to move on and even start dating, and I'd thought perhaps, this was "The Universe," sending me a signal that the time was right. I was planning to spread the remainder of Bob's ashes in a few weeks.

It was July 7, 1997 when Gillian, one of Bob's longest friends, joined Mom and I on a little hike through the beach at Andrew Molera in Big Sur. It's where Bob wanted to be laid to rest. We found a spot on the bluffs overlooking the cove. I spread out some flower seeds, his remaining ashes and the hair we had snipped from Scout's tail. Volume I of the tapes played in the background. We were there over an hour, looking at the scenery and sharing

our thoughts and memories, while being surrounded
by butterflies.

It was emotional, but it also felt like a huge step forward
with a feeling of letting go. It had been over two years since
I'd had sex or even thought about anyone other than Bob.
It was almost as if that two-year mark closed a chapter and
made it possible to start a new one.

## Chapter Two
# TRANSITION

## MASSIVE CHANGES

### Career

After two years, my life was ready for some changes. Massive changes. I could no longer keep doing what I was doing and get better. I wanted to get better, and the insanity of doing the same things over again expecting a different result wasn't working.

I started writing my first draft of *"On Grief and Recovery, One Man's Journey"* (the original title).

It was also around this time that Jessy suggested I work with her again. She moved on from the Bank after it was sold and had begun consulting with a software company. As she explained the position, it sounded like a great fit and I began looking at a career change.

The company was based in Little Rock, though the team I was trying to join was based in Charlotte. I sent my resume, and was immediately informed it wasn't a match. Jessy, however, had other plans and convinced Andrew, the VP of the team, to meet with me. "Trust me, he can do this job. You are not just letting him get away," she later told me she said.

I had one opportunity to interview when he traveled
to Los Angeles on October 1st and I drove down to meet
him. They weren't planning on hiring right away, but were
looking to add head count in the new year, so it could be
a few months before I heard back. Five weeks later, Jessy
called me. "They said you're a keeper! You'll probably get an
offer soon."

"Soon" wound up being another four weeks. On
December 3rd, 1997, I received the offer.

I gave the Credit Union three weeks' notice, and my
last day was December 24, 1997. I started working for
ALLTEL Consulting Services in January 1998. The new
job promised a lot of opportunities to share my expertise
and to travel the world. It was the radical change my life
needed. And it came with a much larger salary. I would
be working as a consultant to banks on business processes
and the integration of technology in those processes. I
have been preparing for years with various positions in
the banking industry to become an expert, to the point of
developing a proprietary methodology and adapting it to
our business practice.

In addition to the salary, the massive change, the
opportunity to use my expertise, a big part of the reason
I took the job was because of the promise of travel,
the opportunity for me to see the world. Thailand was
mentioned. Europe was mentioned. The southeastern
part of the United States was not, though that's where the
company was headquartered.

## Dating

Around the same time I was looking at a career change, I felt it was time to start dating, but I hadn't dated in nearly 10 years and had, for all intents and purposes, pushed most my local friends away in my grief, especially many of those shared friends that would bring back memories. I began looking at the Internet for a place to belong, as many people did back then, and even more nowadays.

One of the first places online that I found where I belonged was the website for the publication for The Advocate, a magazine for the LGBTQ+ community. In the early days of the Internet, several magazine publications hosted forums for discussion. It was here on the forum for "The Advocate," where I honed my arguments for equality and find the research and share the research that being gay was not an issue. We had our fair share of right-wing trolls even then, but I found a community of like-minded people with whom I could discuss current, topical content.

This was also the first place I felt safe enough to talk with other gay men, behind the anonymity of a keyboard. I made friends with several of the regular posters, one of whom with his husband would eventually be the best men at my commitment ceremony.

In August 1997, I found myself falling for one of my fellow keyboard warriors. We didn't exchange pictures, but words. His writing impressed me; his knowledge and passion for any subject matter drew me to him. I don't remember who budged first, but we did eventually exchange email addresses and then finally phone numbers. The more we communicated, the more I was falling for him. Geography would be an issue. I lived in California, he lived in Boston.

But we tried to make it work. We'd speak for hours on the phone and email throughout the day. Twenty-five months and two days after my husband died, I had a new person telling me he loved me. I had yet to meet Troy in person, but I could definitely tell I was falling for him and that frankly scared the hell out of me. I missed my husband, though I know he didn't want me to be alone. We'd talked about this. He wanted me to find someone.

I made plans to meet Troy in Boston, flying out on October 10th. As a native Southern Californian, I had no idea what to expect in Boston. I wasn't prepared for all the colors, though. The leaves were firing orange, red, and yellow. The autumn in full swing as I flew over the city, preparing to land. I didn't know what to expect when I met Troy in person, but when it happened, it felt natural. It felt like we'd known each other for a long time.

We only had a 3-day weekend. He drove me up to Ogunquit, Maine and we stayed in a charming bed and breakfast. We explored a lot of the coastline, and he even drove out to show me the Bush compound in Kennebunkport. Rather, what we could see of the compound from the distance we were. I was introduced to $7 lobsters at a beach-side shack. We drove around marveling at the fall colors. I was enamored. I was in a new place, desperate to tell Bob about it, and realizing he was gone. Conflicted because I was spending a few days with a handsome, passionate man, and grieving my husband. And that was one of the main reasons I was falling for Troy. He understood Bob would always be part of my heart.

But it was also challenging to keep a long-distance relationship going via email and telephone. The more I didn't hear from Troy, the more concerned I was, and the more I missed him. It was tough for me to think about maintaining a relationship with someone that wasn't there next to me.

Troy came to visit me after I had gone through some training in North Carolina in January. I was so excited to have him there, I had to show him off everywhere. He met my family. He met some friends and we met several other Forum friends. I took him to the nursery where Bob used to work to introduce him to the people there. One of them implied the reason for Bob's death was because of AIDS. Once I started dating again, I didn't find the need to disclose my late partner's health history. I was HIV-negative, had been celibate for 2 years, and that's all that mattered in my mind. But Troy felt I kept it from him, and he was very hurt. To further add to his pain, I had created a collage of photos of Bob for his memorial service, and I'd pasted them on a poster board. It had been in my room for two years, and I didn't even think that it would cause Troy any discomfort. It did, and the combination of the two issues both got us to seriously think about this relationship and whether I was ready, or even if he was.

We tried to keep the relationship going for a few months. Still, by the time April rolled around, we'd decided we couldn't make a relationship work. We parted as friends, and remain friends to this day. It hurt me a lot that I caused pain to him. I had a new job I could focus on. I was good at occupying myself with work to get over grief.

I was getting more adept at a dating life in general. I made the most of the fact that I was still relatively young at 31 and sexually active. I accepted opportunities I usually wouldn't have, including a married man. I wasn't immediately aware he was married, with two kids, but he was someone I enjoyed spending time with, whether roller-blading or exploring San Diego. It became clear he was determined to stay in the closet—he had no intention of leaving his wife for me. However, he became more jealous, possessive, and controlling about our relationship. He was beginning to act like I was his property and was expecting me to be there only for him. That's not the kind of relationship I was looking for or wanting, so in today's vernacular, I kicked his ass to the curb and went on my way. One more life lesson for me.

I kissed a few frogs. I was single. Traveling. Employed. I was happy, for the most part. I'd gotten through the heartache from hurting Troy and realized I could actually love someone again. And be loved in return. I found it interesting when I was in one of my training sessions for work that of the 9 men in the class, four were gay. Of the four, there was a mutual attraction with two of them. After a few days of classes, and evenings out with everyone, it became pretty clear that there was some chemistry brewing between Richard and I. We did choose to act on that chemistry. Still, it was also evident that this was another situation that could lead to a long-distance relationship that I wasn't prepared to deal with. Though we did get under each other's skin.

## Lightning Strikes Twice

It had been several months with my new job, and still, the travel was domestic and based in the south. For a native Southern Californian, this may have felt foreign, but it was most definitely domestic. And it was mostly for training. Nearly ten months later, I was finally assigned to a revenue-generating project that would have me working in Memphis for six months. The company put me up in an apartment on the river, a few miles from the customer's office.

I knew I'd be spending months in Memphis. I knew nothing of the city, short of the Blues, BBQ, and Elvis, or it's layout when I arrived, so I plugged my laptop into the phone line, heard the tell-tale SQUEEEEK, EEEERRKKK!!, ZZZHHUUU of the modem connecting to AOL. "You've Got Mail!" the disconnected voice gleefully announced. I navigated to the Memphis page and typed "New in town, will be here a few months. Trying to learn about the city. Anyone up for sharing info and showing me around?"

"I was about to head to church, but I could show you around town."

"Thanks! When and where would you like to meet?"

It was October 4, 1998, when Bob Meek responded to my question. Yes, another man named Bob entering my life. He was 35, blue eyes, a charming smile, and a decent driver. He drove me all over and around the city, pointing out landmarks on Beale Street and places in Germantown. We talked about my job, what I was doing in Memphis, his job, and how he found himself a transplant in Memphis. With the tour over, he said, "I'd like to see you again. Would you like to go on a date Wednesday night?"

Flattered and intrigued, and slightly nervous, I replied, "Yes, Bob. I would like that." I never thought I'd date another guy named Bob. It was the least I could do, and he made me laugh.

## *Chapter Three*
# MY SECOND HUSBAND

## PROLOGUE II

As most of my Fridays have started the last few years, my flight arrived at Boston Logan from San Francisco at around 1:00am. I get home around 2:00am to a quiet house, save for the sounds of Bob snoring loudly in the master bedroom. I don't feel like I want to hear snoring all night, so I choose to sleep in the guest bedroom.

I wake up by 7:00am in the morning, the snoring continuing in the master bed. I get the kids up and out the door for school and take care of the dog's needs. I have a doctor's appointment this morning, so I take a shower and get ready to go. Bob is sleeping peacefully, but the covers are scattered, and it is a cold winter morning. I cover him up, put the dog in the bed to snuggle with him, give him a kiss on the cheek, and leave for my appointment near 8:00am.

I come home around 11:30am. The cleaning ladies are here cleaning, but I don't see Bob anywhere. "He was upstairs sleeping," they tell me.

"That's unusual," I think, "but he has been dealing with the flu." I go upstairs to check on him. What I find is a vision I cannot shake. His lips and face are turning blue. He is no longer snoring. I hear myself screaming, as I lunge to reach him. It is clear he is not responding. I call 9-1-1. I was trained in CPR, but I can't remember what to do. "Put him on the floor," the operator says. "Look for obstruction." I don't see anything. Within minutes, EMTs arrive and usher me aside. "We've got this," they say. I watch in horror.

"Sir, we need to ask you a few questions," I hear. It is an officer from the Police force. "We've seen worse," I hear from the Paramedic. "There's still a chance."

I am led downstairs to the living room to answer the officer's questions. "Did he do drugs?"

"No."

"There's a white powder on the nightstand. Do you know what that could be?"

"No." It turned out to be sugar from sugar cookies. Bob had a sweet tooth.

There are many questions. I can't remember them all, but they feel focused on drugs or suicide.

The Paramedics bring the stretcher downstairs carrying Bob. They are still working on him. There is always a chance. I can't ride with him to the hospital. There are still questions. The Chaplain for the Fire Department arrives. I have to call someone to help with the kids. I hardly know anyone in town. I use Bob's phone and call the first number that shows in history. His friend Karin comes to the house immediately.

"51-year-old white male, possible heart attack, non-responsive, coming in from Lunenburg." Our friend Jaime works in the hospital as a respiratory therapist. She hears the description and the town as the EMT are bringing him into the Emergency Room. She recognizes him immediately.

Still dealing with the police, Karin, the Chaplain, the cleaning ladies also stuck answering questions, and feeling detached from the world, one of the officers enters the living room to tell us Bob has died.

The Chaplain, and Karin, and I talk about what to do with the kids. We will let them complete the day at school but will not allow them to take the bus home. Karin will pick them up. "It's important that you use accurate words," the Chaplain says. "When you tell them, you have to be clear that he died, so they know he's not coming back. And you have to be sure they know you are not going anywhere."

I have to call my Mother-in-Law, Wanda, and tell her that her son is dead. I call. Thankfully, she isn't home—it is a conversation I am able to put off. But I speak with my Father-in-Law, Joe. He will pass the information on.

Jaime leaves work and comes to the house. She and her wife would eventually be extremely helpful in organizing what needed to happen.

Karin calls the school and tells them what is happening. The school holds the kids back while she goes to pick them up. I don't remember who all is in the room when they come home. I focus on them walking in the door with their backpacks on. Young faces showing confusion about why there are people they don't know in our house, and Dad's eyes red and puffy from crying.

Now is the time for the most difficult conversation I've ever had. "Come here," I say, gesturing. "Sit on my lap." They do. "I have some bad news about Daddy Bob. He died today."

"NOOOOOOOOOOOO!!!!!!" is all I hear from our eleven-year-old Abby, a bone-chilling wail. Tears and sobs are coming from ten-year-old Daniel. We all hug each other fiercely.

From that point forward, from January 24, 2014, our lives would never be the same.

## Building a Life Together
### There's Something Happening Here

That first date took us to a brick oven pizza place. We had a good night. We laughed, we enjoyed the food and the company, and I found myself staring at something I'd already gone through with Troy and Richard. I didn't live in Memphis. I had no desire to remain living in Memphis, and while this could be fun, we were still residents of two different states, and I told him, "I am not giving up the job." I liked it. I wanted the travel, the potential journeys, and I liked the fact I could impact positive change in a short time and move on to the next project. He said that didn't scare him.

We wound up spending most of my time in Memphis together outside of work. He and his dog Simba, a purebred Yorkshire Terrier that, I'm told, looked like an Ewok, practically moved into my apartment. Bob introduced me to musical theater by taking me to see *RENT* and *Sunset Boulevard,* with Petula Clark at the Orpheum. These weren't the musicals I recall in the movies from my youth, and I became a fan of the theater and the spectacle and art it provided.

A few weeks after we'd met, I needed to be in Little Rock for meetings with the boss and team. At the same time, I'd started trying to teach myself to play piano. One night, I was using the piano in the lobby of the hotel where I was staying in Little Rock to practice and I was with Jessy when I saw Bob walking in the door. He missed me and drove in from Memphis just to see me.

"That's really sweet," Jessy later told me. "I think you found yourself a keeper." She approved.

By the time Thanksgiving rolled around, he was as much a part of my daily life as he'd ever be. He wanted to introduce me to his family, so we made plans for us to drive up to Indianapolis to meet for Thanksgiving. It's hard enough meeting the family of the person you're dating, but add a major holiday on top of that plus, coincidentally, I was sick with the flu by the time we left. I offered to stay back in Memphis in the apartment, but his mother insisted that it would be OK.

I know myself well enough to know that when I'm sick, I'm not myself, so when I first met Wanda and her husband Joe, Bob's step-father, I couldn't tell what first impression I left. I was shown to my room and told to go lay down, and I did as I was told. Each time I slept at their house, we had separate rooms—I accepted the rule as a necessity knowing the religious background of the request. While loving the sinner, they didn't want us sharing a bed, so I had to respect the rules of the house.

Wanda and I wound up spending a lot of time getting to know each other that weekend. We played cards during any of the free time she had. And she didn't have much. She spent an awful lot of time in the kitchen cooking and baking and she reminded me of a hummingbird... appearing still on the surface, but wings beating incessantly. It was fitting when I learned of her affinity for hummingbirds.

That weekend turned out to be very good. I was welcomed with open arms. I never felt judged. The food was incredible, and I was with someone I loved for the first major holiday in over 3 years.

It was also around this time I'd noticed an unusual growth on my chest. Having already lived through "unusual growths" with my late husband, I was concerned. I went to my doctor and they removed the growth for a biopsy. I had a small hole in my chest, but a huge fear that it was something that was going to kill me. "Maybe they were right," I thought. "Maybe gays just don't live long." I had seen the devastation caused by chemotherapy and vowed never to use it if I wound up with cancer.

I was going to die. Of that, I was certain. But, I learned two weeks later that it was a benign, non-cancerous growth. "I was going to break up with you," I told him. "I'd never want to put you through what I went through."

"I would have been very angry if you pushed me away when you needed me. I'm sad you felt I couldn't."

My birthday in December was supposed to include a horse-drawn carriage, something romantic he'd planned. But that day, I wound up waiting with him in a hospital while he suffered from appendicitis. After months in the hospital with my first Bob (for the sake of clarity going forward, I'll refer to him as Bob1), this was really the last place I wanted to be, but following my own health scare a few weeks prior, it's where I was needed.

Having ridden out that first hospitalization, our first Christmas in the apartment included his putting up a tree and our exchanging gifts. Knowing he was a child at heart, and a Disney fan, I gave him a bouncing Tigger. "Tiggers like to bounce!"

We enjoyed the sights and sounds of the Starry Nights at Shelby Farms Park, driving through and seeing thousands of lights on hundreds of displays. I was actually in the mood to celebrate the season because he made me happy. What were the odds I'd fall for two self-described "Christmas Freaks?"

In January, Bob joined me in California. I introduced him to my friends from the Forum, and a few of the members of my Grief Group. I introduced him to my Mom and Karen. Both were concerned that I was moving too fast, that I wasn't over Bob1. The inevitable comparisons would start: Bob1 was so open and down-to-earth, Bob was on guard; Bob1 was more masculine than Bob2. I didn't know what I expected, but I hoped there would be more of a connection. I chalked it up to the fact that I'd lost the love of my life and they didn't believe I was over him. Neither of them thought I was ready for another relationship.

Four months into the relationship, he proposed to me on Valentine's Day. Between the fear and excitement, I agreed to marry him. The fact I was willing to share my life with someone full-time seemed to happen quickly, especially for our friends and families. In reality, it had actually taken me three years to get to that point. My family, in particular, had a hard time with it. Time would tell if those bridges would ever be mended and crossed.

My first paid assignment ended successfully, and I flew home. At the same time, Bob drove his U-Haul across country to Ventura with Simba. He arrived a few days later, got moved in, and we started planning our ceremony. I'd introduced him to friends I'd made in The Advocate forum, both in and out of state. David and Mark would be our Best Men, Mich from Canada, and Tony from New York State would be part of the "wedding" party. June, from my Grief Group, offered to officiate, and everyone in the Group would attend. I was still participating in my Group, as I was still working on my recovery and now navigating a relationship on top of grieving.

"It's too soon," my Mom said. "Why can't you just live together and get used to each other first? Why the big production? It's not even legal!"

"What if we just change the word to 'Ceremony' from 'Wedding'? Does that make it easier?"

"Why do you need to do this anyway?"

"Why did you walk down the aisle with Jim in front of family and friends?" I asked. I reminded her that it was a public declaration of our commitment to each other and we wanted to celebrate that love, and the fact that I was able to love again, with our families and our friends. And while she eventually agreed that I made sense, she was also afraid Bob was going to come between us and the bond we'd built over the years, despite my reassurances that would not happen.

In May, Mom and I took a trip to Mainz Germany to see my grandmother, whom I hadn't seen in over 25 years. I met my uncle and his family for the first time. Between the German I spoke and the English they spoke, we understood each other well. It was fascinating being in Europe for the first time. We toured the city my Mother was born and raised in, and they took me to the church where she was Christened as a baby. It stands as a war memorial now, a bombed-out shell from World War II. I'd heard the stories of American soldier parachuting in my grandparents' yard with chocolate for the kids and my Mother being terrified at her young age. There were always stories.

Mainz am Rhein is across the Upper Rhine River from Wiesbaden, where an American base is located. This is where my Mother met my father. My Mother told me her birth father was a famous artist before, but he'd died when she was an infant after a surgery. Her mother, my Omi, eventually remarried the man we'd know as Opa. I'd only met him one time when he traveled to the U.S. when I was five-years-old. He was gruff with a peculiar wave that looked like he was flipping us off, that connection made later as I got older. Mom told us stories about him when we were adults that made me glad he was dead by the time I visited Germany.

It was a great bonding trip. One that helped close some chapters in both our lives, and create some new memories and closeness she was afraid of losing. Mom would go back to Germany in August and be there when my Omi died. I'm thankful I had the chance to see her before then... none of us realized she'd be gone a mere three months after leaving.

On the Summer Solstice of 1999, June 21, I made the difficult decision to let go of Soph. My sweet girl had been with me for 11 years, giving me unconditional love and comfort, especially after Bob1 died. Many tear-filled nights were met with snuggles and licks on my face. But she was succumbing to cancer, and letting her go was the only humane thing to do. Bob was there and comforted me, and my irrational mind went back to Scout dying, then Bob1 thinking, "I'm next." I dreamed of her that night, all better, playing with me.

As the day of the ceremony got closer, we dug into the details of flowers, cake, decorations, tuxes, gifts to the wedding party, and attendees. And we worked on a secret that would only be revealed during the ceremony itself. We made the walk-through rehearsal dinner the night before, and on October 9, 1999, nearly a year after we met, we were ready to get married in our back yard. And, absolutely, we went overboard. It was, in a lot of ways, a first for both of us.

## From This Moment

Of course, the best-laid plans tend to go awry. Or, as I've said before, God laughs. The temperature that day was over 100 degrees; the house did not have air conditioning. Someone loaded the garbage disposal with tea bags from the iced tea, which clogged the pipes requiring a plumber. I later learned our mothers were apprehensive about being walked down the aisle, and they weren't feeling it. My Mom had to convince Wanda to do it. "I don't necessarily agree with what they're doing, either, but I'm going to be there for my son."

I was upstairs in the master bed, getting dressed, looking out my window to the back yard. The seats on "my side" of the aisle were all in the blaring sun, and I couldn't see anyone sitting there, and I couldn't see the other side of the aisle from my room.

We mustered at opposite sides of the house, each with a gate into the back yard. The processional music played bringing our parents down the aisle and, once seated, *"I do swear, That I will always be there. I'd give anything and everything, and I will always care..."* our voices exploded from the speakers as we sang Shania Twain's *"From This*

*Moment"* to each other while walking up the side of the house and down the aisle. It was a special moment, one that caught our guests off guard and talked about for years to come. I remember during the interlude seeing my Mom crying, and I reached out to her. She squeezed my hand and smiled, and in that moment I thought everything was going to be alright. And even though, at this point in time, the ceremony wasn't legal (registered domestic partnership notwithstanding), it was something we felt necessary to do in front of friends and family.

From that moment on, after the ceremony was complete, and we pledged our lives together, we did what we needed to do to honor those vows. My career was excelling, Bob was working in a career he enjoyed until a particular boss made it unenjoyable. He eventually left the job and took a position in retail, with IT jobs being scarce in the area. One day, he re-inflamed an old injury in his back from when he was an EMT. Surgery was required to fix the issue, but the scar tissue kept him in constant pain and unable to work.

Nearly three years later, the honeymoon phase had played out, and the dynamics of our relationship had changed. Having gained some success on projects at work, I was sought-after. I was traveling nearly every week to client sites. My frequent absences and the lack of employment on his side led to some destructive choices, and when I'd discovered that he'd been sleeping with other men, I confronted him about it.

I no longer remember if it was email or AOL chat, but he left a window open on his computer once and I saw the evidence of at least one encounter, and it had been with a mutual friend of ours.

"What the hell is this? Do you want to explain this?"

"You're never here! I have needs that aren't being met!"

"And you think mine are when I'm gone all the time? And with HIM?!" I'd considered the guy a friend, but I couldn't imagine a friend would do something like that to me.

This was unusual territory for me, having come from a monogamous relationship with Bob1, and I recognized the difference in this relationship versus the first. As I struggled with this new dynamic and new information, I had a decision: was the relationship more important than the sex?

"Look, I get that I'm gone a lot. I get that we're both sexual beings. I get that if you're going to continue, then both of us should have that option." He wasn't too keen on that possibility, but I threw it out there, more as a challenge. "If it's OK for you, then it has to be OK for me."

I determined, for me, and for that relationship, where I was gone more than home, I could make an open relationship work. A relationship has to be built on more than the physical and, in my mind, the physical is but one aspect.

We set ground rules around any encounters we might have, which included the use of condoms, and no "dating." Again, this was unusual to me but made sense for us at the time.

## Becoming Parents

Also, around this time, Bob heard an ad on the radio station about the County seeking foster parents for an ever-increasing need. I'd always wanted to have children, but I never thought it possible once I admitted I was gay. I thought gay people don't have children and, if they did, you certainly didn't see them in the 1980s or 1990s.

But they did. And the County did not discriminate based on marital status or sexual orientation, so we thought long and hard on it. Could we really become parents? Was this really something we wanted to do? Was this in the best interests of any potential children? Our parents thought we were crazy and terrified that people would think we were "recruiting" or molesting children. This is what they were taught. Gay people are pedophiles. This, despite the evidence proving it's simply not the case, and most pedophiles are heterosexual opportunists.

We eventually decided in early 2002 to become Foster/Adopt parents, meaning we could foster children and adopt if the parental rights were terminated through the judicial process. We had to complete two applications (one of each agency) and undergo background checks and training. Meanwhile, two teenagers fondling themselves in the backseat of their parent's Buick could just make a baby without any training. I felt, in a way, that we would be more "qualified" to be parents by going through this and wondered why parenting classes weren't mandatory in school curricula.

Our foster parent mentor was a straight, married, Catholic woman. She fell in love with Bob (who was primarily home as I was, as usual, traveling) and helped him navigate through the process. She mentored him to become a mentor, and he recruited other same-sex couples to become foster or adoptive parents. We held Dad's group meetings at our home to discuss the challenges of the process, and eventually, the challenges of parenting as a father in society.

Simple things like changing tables in the men's restrooms at restaurants. There were so few at that time, we would wind up changing diapers on the sink or on our laps or, sometimes, in the booth in which we were sitting.

Or, how do we address when someone says, "Oh, it must be dad's day out with the kids giving Mom a break!" Answers varied from "let it go" to "confront." Our preferred method was to "educate," "No Mom involved. We're raising her together." Sometimes, it led to a dialogue, other times we were congratulated for doing so, and on rare occasions, we heard, "that's so wrong."

I found myself in a more spiritual space by that point, having given up on organized religion years ago when I nearly died. That experience left me with peace, and I found organized religion had been a weapon used to demonize me and others that were "different." I've known atheists that had more compassion and behaved more "Christ-like" than some self-described "Christians." And I never cottoned to the idea that one church's beliefs made one more inclined to receive Heavenly praise. To be clear, I am not anti-Christian or anti-any religion; I believe that faith is personal and where one finds comfort in their soul is not for me to judge.

So, when it came time to raise our children, we did so without an organized religion behind us. We celebrated mainly Christian holidays, but also informed the kids there were other religions and other methods of worship and beliefs. We didn't want to "indoctrinate," but rather inform and allow them to ask questions and investigate on their own. This helped when world religions were discussed in school history classes.

By mid-2002, we'd completed all the checks and all the home visits and got our license. Within hours of completing the licensure, we received the first call for an older sibling group that we weren't able to take on immediately. Within a few weeks, we participated in the Foster Parents' Father's Day Picnic. From the moment we arrived, our mentor Patti had placed a 2.5-month-old baby girl in our arms. It felt as if we were test-driving infants.

In a way, we were. She was so small, with chubby cheeks and dark hair with greenish-hazel eyes, and she looked at me with her toothless grin, and my heart melted. So did Bob's. Patti saw this and said, "this is your daughter. On Monday, you need to call the agency and ask to have her placed with you." She gave us the information we needed and told us she'd call the County as well. "Are you sure they're ready?" we heard they'd asked her. "Oh, yes. They're ready."

On June 14, our daughter was placed into my arms as one of her foster dads. In my family, she was the first granddaughter. Her birth family was from the same county and town, and we'd heard from our mentor that they had several other children in the system and they knew a lot of people. She had a unique name at birth that, if we'd used in public, could lead the birth family to us, and we weren't prepared for that or an open adoption, if it came to that, and we thought of names for her. We also knew the likelihood that her birth parents would fight for custody, as they had for their other children.

Bob always liked the name Abigail. It was unique in Southern California, too, and it sounded classic. We looked it up for its meaning and found it meant "A Father's Joy." We thought she was our joy, and that sounded like a good fit. "What about the middle name, though?"

We fumbled through several incarnations of Abigail Denise, Abigail Grace, Abigail Rose, etc., and we finally settled on Abigail Renee. Renee means "to be reborn." We were so scared and so proud. We almost immediately gathered my family at a restaurant half-way between us, to introduce her. And she was everything we expected between the giggles and the midnight or 2:00am feedings. But it didn't matter. We were dads and we couldn't be happier.

The requirements of my job, however, remained the same. There was still a lot of traveling, and, for all intents and purposes, Bob was a single parent most weekdays. He was a stay-at-home dad, the medical disability still making it impossible for him to stand or sit for hours. I started noticing more withdrawals from the checking account; Bob was not afraid of shopping and I frequently came home to something new in the house. What I didn't realize, over the course of a few months, was that in addition to the material things, Bob had also been doctor shopping. I began noticing multiple withdrawals of several hundred dollars coming out of the account.

When I confronted him with the bank information about the pharmacy charges, he broke down and confessed to what was going on: he was addicted to opioids. In an effort to control the pain, he'd been filling Vicodin prescriptions online, to the point where he was taking 30 pills per day to manage. But it wasn't just to manage the pain, it was also to manage the loneliness he felt with my being gone so much, and to manage the chaotic demands of parenting. He would quit using, and he'd seek counseling to deal with the emotional pieces of the reason for his addiction. He went to his mother's house to get clean. He would look for other methods of pain management that did not involve opioids.

While he was using, and before I'd realized there was an addiction, we had visited my parents with our daughter and another foster child. My Mother had been holding Abby's hand while she toddled. Bob saw something and berated my Mom, "WE don't do that!" He became unreasonable, and my Mom put up her defenses. She is not one to be treated that way, and the addiction left a rift between him and my family that never healed fully. And it caused pain in our relationship to the point where I was talking about divorce. I wouldn't tolerate that behavior and recklessness, especially around my child.

There was more soul-searching and living differently than I'd been used to, however, Bob2 and I had some of the same communication issues Bob1 and I had experienced. We learned this is common among couples. I had to decide whether this relationship was worth keeping. I'd modified my values on monogamy to accommodate, and that seemed to be OK. Was this relationship worth working on? I had made a promise after singing down an aisle with him. I didn't say I'd only be there during good times, and this was definitely not a good time. So, I decided we needed to work on this together, and we went to couple's counseling in addition to his personal counseling. And we learned how to communicate again.

We learned that we both shared some resentment about the other in the way our relationship, and the family we were building, was taking place. I was making good money, but I still looked for local opportunities. He resented I was gone all the time, I resented I was gone all the time. But I enjoyed the job, and I kept advancing in the company as a valued resource.

In the meantime, Abby's birth parents were fighting to keep her, which certainly caused some stress. The goal of foster parenting is to provide a safe space for the child while allowing parents the time and education needed to get themselves together to the satisfaction of the courts and to allow for the reunification of the family. Given the family's history with the County, it was highly unlikely they would be reunified. However, the goal remained, and the parents had legal rights to work to maintain their parental rights.

In late November 2003, I was working in Chicago with a large financial institution. I'd spent weeks going back and forth between San Diego, home, and Chicago. I made a practice of calling home every night to check on Bob and Abby. One night, Bob told me, "I've been having an affair with the mailman, and we now have a son."

I knew he was joking about the affair, and my immediate response was, "WE don't have a son unless I agree, you know." He proceeded to tell me about the week-old infant in our home, with his wild hair and huge eyes.

I flew back home a few days later, and I held my son for the first time. I'd always wanted a son. I wanted to do dad/son things that I never got to do with my absent father. That's one thing the bastard taught me, how to be a better father than he was. I'd had the name William Michael for a boy in my pocket for years, but when I looked at this tiny Latino bundle, he didn't look like a William. And we wanted to honor his heritage. After much thought, we chose Daniel Miguel as his name. And we welcomed him into the house, into our hearts, and into the family.

Contrasting Abby's birth parents, Daniel's birth parents did not fight to retain custody. By serendipity, the parental rights of both were terminated around the same time, and we were able to adopt both on the same day. On October 15, 2004, with a 2½ year and an 11-month-old, we made it official. We gathered in the Family Court, waiting for our turn before the judge. My parents and sister came, Bob's parents came, many local friends, including several members of my Grief Group and Jessy came, other foster-to-adopt parents came, and Troy came with his husband from Boston. When it was our turn, we entered the courtroom. I held Daniel, Bob held Abby.

The Judge asked us questions. Were we ready? Did we know what this meant? Etc. We repeatedly answered in the affirmative, "Yes." Our toddler, however, having a new favorite word repeatedly answered, "No." When the Judge asked Abby if she wanted a teddy bear, the "No" quickly turned to "Yes," and the gallery laughed. We gathered at our home and even more people showed up, including Gillian, the old friend with Bob1. It was one of the most important days of my life.

The next year or so would take me to North Carolina for a long-term project. The customer put me up in an extended day hotel. Eventually, I brought Bob and the kids to North Carolina with me, and they stayed at the hotel with me for weeks at a time. We even had Simba with us. I didn't know what to expect with two gay men raising two babies and being in the south surrounded by churches and co-workers. What I found surprised me. Not a negative comment from anyone around us. In fact, one of my co-workers credits my being open to opening HER eyes to diversity and love. We made some lifelong friendships over nearly two years being there (with some back and forth to California). Abby celebrated her 4th birthday at the hotel in the banquet room. The staff helped set up and joined us in celebration. We put a small tree in our place over Christmas. In September 2005, the project was called off, and we all headed home.

The staff threw a farewell party for all of us that had been staying there all those months. They gave us goodbye presents, and they gave the kids several things. We wound up having to ship several boxes via UPS back home. Still, we were sad to go and more depressed to see the new family we'd created in North Carolina scatter to the wind. The time together was good for us. But eventually, I would be traveling again for work, and I'd be wishing to spend more time with my family.

## Challenges

In June 2006, after 8½ years, I was laid off with about 350 other people in a "right-sizing" operation that found my position was "redundant." It didn't feel redundant when, on the next day, I was contacted by someone from the International side of the company who said, "I hear you're looking for work. Come to Buenos Aires with me." I'd worked with this team before, and I enjoyed the international travel and projects. "OK," I said, "but I'm a contractor now." I then told her my rate, which I tripled from my salary, and she agreed. I could have just transferred and saved them some money, but that option was never presented.

The next few years found me as an independent consultant making many international trips to multiple clients. At the same time, Jessy and I were working on getting a boutique consulting firm off the ground. Our specialty was in helping banks focus their technology investments on process improvement. Our market focus shifted from large financial institutions to community banks. We developed a model that analyzed their reported financial statements and could predict savings if they utilized our services. We were so confident, we guaranteed our work.

And we spent a lot of time doing business development from analysis to marketing to follow-up calls. We advertised, we became members of several organizations, and we presented at a conference in Hawaii. We spent money like we had money, but the runway was long to get any kind of payback, and neither of us seemed to be able to close many deals. We needed a salesperson. The good news was that I was close to home and my family, but the bad news was that I was losing money. When I'd wished to stay home more, I should have been specific that I still wanted to earn a paycheck. It was terribly stressful, and when the opportunity came to work outside of Manchester, England, I took the job. I would spend 4 weeks in-country, and 2 weeks home, for several months. I'd perform the analysis and letter generations for Jessy during the evenings while

I was in the UK, and she would print, mail and follow up with prospects. It worked, and thankfully I was still able to earn a paycheck.

At Bob's prompting, we also started a wedding and event videography company in 2007 as a way to bring money into the house. We had a friend that is an event planner, and he hooked us up to a few weddings. We did the first few for free to have footage we could edit and use for marketing. So I became adept at filming, editing, and photoshop to create content we could use to market.

2008 was a year that changed the world. In California, the Supreme Court ruled in favor of same-sex marriage in the summer. We took advantage of the fact it was our 10th Anniversary from our meeting, so we were legally married 10 years to the day of our meeting.

It was a much smaller affair than the ceremony in 1999. We set up the patio gazebo on the back porch with an altar, music, lighting and flowers. A handful of guests were invited, including Jessy and some long-term friends. Abby was the flower girl, and Daniel, the ring bearer. Another friend who was ordained performed the small ceremony. Abby, now 6, wore a tiara, gently tossing rose petals. Daniel, almost 5, followed her with the box of rings and a fauxhawk hairstyle. Bob and I followed, holding hands as we heard the familiar song of Shania Twain's *"From This Moment."* I joked there would be no signing this time. After the ceremony, we danced together and with our children. Never in my life had I expected that I would be legally married to another man.

Following the Court's ruling in California, there was a fierce battle for the November election with Proposition 8, which would ban marriage equality in the state, on the ballot. The passage of Proposition 8 on the same night as President Obama's victory stung, though. I found it hard to believe the majority of my fellow citizens were progressive enough to vote for Obama, but not enough to defeat a ban on same-sex marriage.

Also in October, 2008, everything was changing across the globe. The Great Recession took hold, and nobody was willing to spend money on consultants. Our leads dried up. Though we knew this was the perfect time for banks to adjust how they did business, we couldn't get a call back. My latest contract with a bank in the UK was not renewed, and I spent the next 9 months unemployed, not for lack of trying. I spent hours every day combing through employment opportunities in the local paper and online. I applied for literally anything that I had a skill-set for, but nothing was coming. I called all my old contacts, I applied for temporary work and had little luck even there. Unemployment ran out quickly and then the 401(k) withdrawals had to be made, knowing I'd be paying a hefty penalty for doing so. On the verge of filing bankruptcy, with multiple charge-offs on my record, I found a consulting gig in New Orleans. Unlike other contracts I'd become accustomed to 9 months ago, this one did not pay for travel or lodging.

## New Orleans / New Chapter

In July 2009, I packed up my Prius and drove to New Orleans on short notice. It took 3 days and 5 tanks of gas, but I made it through the freak thunderstorms of Arizona and the 80 MPH highway in Texas. I couldn't even get from one end of Texas to the other before spending the second night in Houston during another downpour. I literally didn't have a place to stay when I arrived in the Crescent City. I had to borrow money from my Mother to get an apartment. Using Craigslist when I got there, I found a quiet, furnished apartment in the Garden District on the second floor. I was not prepared for the frequent storms (my car was flooded twice) or the extreme humidity. Still, I was able to successfully work on a complete re-design of a bank's loan origination process. Every bank likes to think they're unique, but with the regulations required, there's not much possible variation. So, in order for a bank to feel they are unique, they usually claim to have a "secret sauce," which is some cases is simply the way in which they treat, or segment, their customers.

It would be a few months before I could go home. I was maintaining two households and worked both for the bank and on wedding video editing. I was burned out, stressed, and feeling guilty about leaving my family. The relationship challenges kept popping up, whether it was his spending, his not doing editing, my not being there, or the open relationship. But I did what I could to keep the family fed and housed and intact. We were even approached by a casting director to be included on the TV show "The Marriage Ref," which was a vehicle of Jerry Seinfeld's that didn't last long. We were desperate to raise funds and keep the relationship going, and by the time we saw the show air, we were glad not to have been part of it. Though at that point, $5,000 could have helped a lot.

Bob was good at selling the videography services and made the couples feel at ease. We had worked with the Amway Corporation in the early 2000's, when they were rebranding themselves as Quixtar, and we really enjoyed the positivity and camaraderie. He tried his hand at several different multi-level-marketing opportunities to bring some money in, one of which provided some benefits to help his pain (Xango) and another because he liked collecting pretty things (PartyLite).

## Working on Us

We had a lot of things going both for and against us. In the "For" column, we had our commitment and love for each other and our children. We were pretty solid, despite some issues and struggles. He was in constant pain and an opioid addict, so managing his physical pain was challenging. I was never home and getting fatter. Intimacy was pretty much off the table because I couldn't deal with my negative body image and he wasn't attracted to my weight gain, so we both sought it elsewhere. I felt I worked a lot, sometimes too much, to make sure my family had the resources to get by and prosper and recover from the near bankruptcy. He liked shopping and spending money. When I was home, I felt like the novelty parent to my six- and seven-year-old, and he resented that he'd spend all week, or weeks, in a routine, and I'd be home a few days and upend everything. I would upset nighttime routines by later "family movie nights." I'd take the kids to the park and play, or we'd go out and do something "exciting" versus the routine day-to-day stuff they were used to.

There were times where we talked about getting divorced. Neither of us felt our needs being met. There was a lot of resentment in both directions over the perceptions of what the other had. And living in different cities was not helping the matter. Still, we decided that it wouldn't be fair to the kids or to us if we didn't try to get through some of the issues that were pushing us apart. We both sought individual counseling and couples counseling. Anyone that's been married knows that it's work, and you have to do the work to reap the rewards. And we worked. We came up with plans to help each of the issues, and we tried.

One of the biggest issues we faced was in our finances. I worked trying to maintain two households, and we were still scraping by paycheck-to-paycheck. He collected some disability. It felt as though I was the only one making sacrifices in the finances. I didn't buy anything that wasn't necessary. I had to keep a close eye on the bank account given his past, and he resented that I would question every withdrawal. His mother had a suggestion I thought worth trying: give him a cash allowance each week that he could do what he wanted with and I didn't have to see the transactions coming into the account. It made life more bearable for me, and he didn't feel like I was micro-managing him.

The economy started picking up in my industry in late 2009, and full-time jobs were becoming available. I was approached by an international corporation looking for a project manager with years of banking experience to help define a banking solution for North America. As cautious as I am, I assumed it was a scam to take advantage of someone struggling in the economy. Despite my successes, I couldn't believe a large international corporation would reach out to me. But it was not a scam, and we started talking. At the same time, the employer that had released me with my 350 co-workers contacted me and asked if I'd like to come back and work in their Project Management Office. I entertained both options. I went through three interviews with the first company, finishing with the VP of Financial Services and one more to go before they would decide. I went through two meetings with my former employer. After this second interview, they offered me a full-time position. I called the first company and told them I had an offer on the table. I let them know that if they were seriously considering me, they would need to expedite the last interview since I had 48 hours to provide a response to the offer. The first company rallied, and we finished the interviews with an offer that was 50% higher than my prior employer.

No brainer, right? Wrong. I didn't know this first company. I knew their reputation, but I had no idea what I would be stepping into, I couldn't support the product since I've never touched their software. Then, on the other hand, there was the Devil I knew. I knew I was able to support the product. I knew the organization's processes, and I knew that the prior 8½ years of revenue generation meant nothing to them when it came down to it. As I was striving to correct the mess that was my life, I was also working with a life coach. He got me thinking about scenarios for each of the opportunities presented to me with this significant decision. Rather than a pros and cons list, we took a different view and went a little deeper with some neurolinguistic programming: What would happen if I said YES to this offer? What would happen if I said NO? What would NOT happen if I said YES? What would NOT happen if I said NO?

We worked on the questions, I consulted with Bob, and then I made a decision. Nothing ventured, nothing gained. I chose to go with the first company and not my former employer. My time in New Orleans was coming to an end, and hopefully, a difficult chapter in our lives would also come to an end. The decision called for a celebration of epic proportions, and nothing was quite as epic as Mardi Gras in New Orleans.

The family flew out for Mardi Gras, Bob and I hired a sitter and hit the parades and Bourbon Street. I'd been living in this city for eight months, completely taken in by the culture and the people, witnessing the devastation left by Hurricane Katrina that still marred much of the Crescent City. In 2005, while I was working in Rocky Mount, several of us were planning a weekend trip to New Orleans. It was to have been my first time in NOLA. Bob was letting me get away and have some fun with the team. But then, Katrina formed and devastated the city on that weekend.

I saw the rise, and the ultimate victory, of the New Orleans Saints in the Super Bowl. It was impossible not to get drawn into the joy of the city and their team. During the daytime with the kids, we visited many of the family-friendly parades. The huge floats and decorations and the beads all captured the kids' attention. They quickly learned how to get the attention for the throws, including an unopened bag of beads that landed on Abby's head. Once Mardi Gras 2010 was complete, the family flew home, and it was my turn to take that cross-country drive by myself.

The Prius was packed again, this time with a few more things I'd acquired in the 8 months, plus at least 75 pounds of throws collected by the kids that Bob wanted to keep for a "Mardi Gras Christmas Tree" stuffed in the back seat floorboard. On February 17th, I started my drive home.

## The Move
The next year or so brought much of the same in terms of travel, work, and frustrations from both. But we made it

work. We learned how to communicate better and express what we needed we felt was missing. We were beginning to rebuild the finances that took a beating, and the State of California was about to implement some changes that would have had a disastrous effect on our finances. I was working on the east coast, traveling back and forth weekly. Bob was missing the seasons after 12 years in Southern California. The kids were getting older, soon needing their own space, and California real estate, where we lived, wasn't getting any more affordable. Everything aligned and pointed us to a decision I never thought I'd have to make: it makes sense to leave my home state and my home, and move somewhere out of state. The question then became "where?"

In 2011, a handful of states recognized same-sex marriage, which was paramount in our decision-making because, wherever we decided to go, our familial relationship and our children's rights had to be respected. We agreed on Massachusetts for several reasons and set about looking for a new homestead. Since I was traveling and not home much, my primary criteria included the proximity to an airport. Good schools, diverse, and affordable were all considerations. The further we expanded the search from Logan Airport, the more affordable the options became, even though they were also less diverse. Being a resident of Massachusetts, and familiar with the state, Troy offered to help us find a place, and Bob flew out to begin the search.

It wouldn't take long before Bob found what he was looking for. It was an old Victorian built in 1895 with original flooring, rooms for each of the kids, an office we could work out of, a pool, huge maple trees, a wrap-around porch, and a community that felt rural and hometown-ey. The schools were excellent, and we could move from our 1,351 square foot home in California to a nearly 2,500 square foot home in Massachusetts for the same amount. The house had only been with one family since it was built, and the seller was willing to hold paper while we rebuilt our credit from the 2008 economy. The stars fell into place, and we moved across the country in June of 2011. The week after we moved, and as I'd expected because God laughs, I received a call from my boss about my next assignment located a mere 40-minute drive away... from our old home in California.

On the plus side of cross-country traveling, I was able to spend some weekends in California visiting with my family. The possibility of the move convinced my Mom she'd never see me again, and that Bob was taking me away from her. Their relationship never fully recovered, despite a few attempts by both of them to bury the hatchet. In reality, I probably saw her and my sister more after I'd moved to Massachusetts than when I lived a four-hour drive away. It was hard to visit when I was only home one full day per weekend. I spent the next few years traveling back and forth between the Bay Area, home, and northern France. I was working with a team of innovators taking new technologies we'd developed and expanding into predictable analytics and doing some cutting-edge work. It was fascinating and frustrating as hell, and I was making a name for myself. I was being courted to move into a new division within the company, but I'd have to move back to California. That wasn't something I was willing to do without some substantial concessions, and moving allowance they couldn't meet. So I continued my cross-country and cross-Atlantic journeys racking up points for hotels and flights. I was Platinum status and enjoyed the extra perks that entailed, like upgrades and point bonuses, early boarding, fee waivers and drinks.

Bob built a life in Lunenburg, becoming a fixture in the Schools and the PTO. He made friends easily and was quickly accepted into the community. Bob ran for School Committee after a few years and worked with a group of people to get a new school built for the Middle/High School. He was making a name for himself in the town.

I was away from my family more than I'd been before, and it was time to use those earned points to make some memories with them. The odds were that someday, the traveling was going to literally kill me. I'd already been exposed to Tuberculosis on one of the trips for which I'd been successfully treated. So I used the points I racked up to plan a once-in-a-lifetime, memory-building vacation with my family. In August 2013, I booked first-class seats to London for us and explored the city I had been working in. We went to Warwick Castle to see the world's largest functioning trebuchet. We visited the Warner Brothers' *Harry Potter* lot; with a 9 and 11-year-old, it was as magical and entertaining as the books and movies had been for me. Daniel became adept at navigating the Tube. We took a train to Paris, where Bob and I relived some romantic times, but also shared the Eiffel Tower, Notre Dame, and the Catacombs with the kids. We took an overnight train through the Alps to arrive in Firenze, Italy. I fell in love with the city earlier in the year, and I introduced them to *il Duomo,* Buca Mario's, the Gold Bridge, and *il Porcellino.* We drove out to Pisa and the coast, and returned home again snuggled in first-class, forever spoiling the children for traveling. It was definitely a trip to remember, and I felt great to be able to make these memories with my kids and my husband.

But four months later, I'm the one left with the memories. I'm left with a life that looks nothing like it did. I'm left as a single parent trying to make sense of it all. I'm grieving my second husband, which I never expected to be doing. ***I was the one that was supposed to go first.***

*Robert Harold Meek-LaVeck*
*November 8, 1962–January 24, 2014*

## Grief and Recovery
### The Memories
Well over a hundred people in this small community of 10,000 attended his memorial service. It was standing room

only. I heard stories about a man that I didn't really know. I knew the husband. I knew the father. But he presented a different persona to others. They knew the funny jokester. They knew the "fun" Bob. He integrated himself in this community quickly, and deeply. I was and remain moved by the support the community showed us, merely by being his family.

We held the service in February, on a Saturday, to allow the school community to attend. He'd become close with many of the teachers and parents and staff at the schools, and several members reached out to me about wanting to be sure they could come. Bob's mom, brother and sister-in-law came to visit. My sister represented my family; my Mom was no longer comfortable flying. We hired a photographer to capture moments, and a videographer to capture the service. One of Bob's friends took photos and made a music video slide-show which played on a loop as we all gathered, Pentatonix singing *"Run To You"* and Josh Groban's *"The Prayer"* with Charlotte Church. I hired a non-denominational reverend to officiate.

One neighbor spoke of the first time meeting him, in his Obama t-shirt, and wondering who he was after we'd moved in. They became very close. Karin spoke of her friend, and the lunches or ice cream runs they would take. One of Karin's sons read a letter Daniel wrote, but didn't feel comfortable delivering to an audience. Abby surprised me by getting up to speak about her dad. Again and again, friends and family went to the podium to speak of their love for my husband. Similar to the last time, I don't know how I managed to read my eulogy:

*It was 15 years ago and I was new in the world of consulting, expecting a long-term assignment in Memphis, and tentatively breaking free from a three-year mourning phase, when I met and was immediately drawn to Bob. His humor, child-like exuberance and charm drew me in. Two months after we started dating, I wound up taking him to the hospital with appendicitis. I never did get that horse-drawn carriage ride for my birthday and I reminded him each year.*

*It wasn't long before he started keeping things in my apartment and when he proposed on Valentine's Day in 1999, I was probably as stunned as anyone else. I said yes, he moved to California – he liked to tell the story of how I made him drive across country in a U-Haul while I flew.*

*It's hard to believe that a little more than 14 years ago, that October day in 1999 in the heat of Southern California, we gathered a few dozen friends in our small backyard. We surprised them with a duet of "From This Moment" as we started our commitment ceremony walking down the aisle. We made promises then, to love and respect, honor and cherish and to be there for each other in the good and bad times, until death do us part. We did so not with the weight or enforcement of law, but because that's what we needed to do to seal our commitment to one another in our eyes and in the eyes of our friends and families.*

*By 2002, we decided we wanted to be parents and we began the process of becoming foster and adoptive parents. This is where Bob began with his advocacy for children by getting involved in the Ventura County Foster Parents Association. After adopting Abby and Daniel, he remained active in the Foster Parenting movement and recruited several adoptive parents. He advocated for our children with the schools and doctors. I have two pretty amazing kids in Abby and Daniel, and I credit Bob for working so hard to raise them as they are. He was absolutely a fierce advocate for children until his death.*

*He brought this advocacy with him when we moved to Lunenburg 2½ years ago. Choosing Lunenburg was fairly random. We were ready to leave California and Bob wanted seasons, we needed someplace that recognized the legality of our family and New*

*England was progressive enough to meet those needs. We knew two people in town when we relocated and the schools seemed to fit the needs of the kids.*

*And so it came to be that Bob became a fixture at the schools, the PTO and the new school supporters. I knew Bob was involved in our community, but I honestly did not comprehend the breadth and depth of his involvement. I could not have known the impact he had, and will have, on this community. And this community will never fully understand the impact they have had on me and the kids since Bob died. There is so much gratitude we have that I cannot adequately express in words how thankful we are.*

*I grieve for the future lost, the moments we will not get to have. I worry about how this will impact my children and our families. At 51, he was too young.*

*The Dalai Lama said, "There are only two days in the year that nothing can be done. One is called yesterday and the other is called tomorrow, so today is the right day to love, believe, do and mostly live."*

*I got 15 pretty good years with Bob. He did a great job working on raising our kids.*

*He made it known to us how much we were*
*loved by him. He made solid friends and*
*had a chosen family here in Lunenburg. We*
*can't forget what he meant to us, and so we*
*can honor him by continuing to advocate for*
*the children of this town. We can greet each*
*other with kindness and a smile. We can give*
*our kids an extra tight hug and extra word of*
*encouragement. We can remember the smile,*
*the laugh and the bright blue eyes. And we can*
*recall how he impacted our lives and we can*
*pay it forward. He will be missed, but he will*
*not be forgotten.*

*"Those we love don't go away. They*
*walk beside us every day. Unseen, unheard*
*but always near. Still loved, still missed and*
*very dear."*

As anyone who's lost anyone can attest, the first weeks were a blur. That I was able to function at all is a mystery. Though I do know that without the friends Bob had made while I was off earning a living and making a career, it would have been impossible. And so, unlike 1995, when all I wanted was to be left alone, I'd remembered that lesson and allowed people to help me. I didn't have to go through it alone. And I wasn't the only one grieving. Friends and family lost someone they loved, too, and if it helped them heal and feel better to provide a meal to us, I wasn't going to deny them that opportunity to help. The technological advances between deaths allowed for a coordinated effort of people to prepare and drop off meals to the point where I don't think I had to cook for well over 2 months. It allowed me to focus on maintaining my health and the kids'. I am thankful for the help.

I was suddenly thrust into single-parenthood, in a community where I had no family to help, but Bob's friends were here. They helped not only with feeding us but also with the immediate need for scheduling services and dealing with creditors, lawyers, etc. I could no longer travel for work, and my employer did what they could to allow me to work from home. It was about 6 months before they'd tell me travel was part of my job description, so I had time to find something else either internally or leave. I managed to find something temporarily within the company for a year, then found a full-time position within the company that allowed me to work entirely remotely. I have been with this company for 10 years. I think back to the bidding war for me in late 2009, the choice between the Devil I knew and the Devil I didn't know. I wonder how the Devil I knew would have treated me, and I am thankful for the choice I made.

Having a feeling of thankfulness is challenging to find in the middle of chaos, and my life was chaotic. Soon to have a house full of family and friends for Bob's service, still pending details on the cause of death, children unable to sleep in their own beds and always needing assurances, and my inability to sleep at all because of the stress. This time around, I knew drinking myself to sleep was not an option. I was a parent. Every move forward would be modeling behavior for my kids on how to navigate the death of a loved one, and how to manage grief and recovery. I had to teach them that crying, showing emotion, was OK. I had to teach them that speaking of your loved one is OK, that it helps keep the memory alive and reminds us that they are still part of us.

It dawned on me, in the middle of this horrific second time of rebuilding my life and dealing with my husband's death, that I was thankful to have been through this already. I had a road map, I knew what to expect, I knew what didn't work, and more importantly, I knew what would work for me. Even when the stress was overwhelming, and the relationship on the rocks, I'd spent the last several years trying to be thankful daily for something good in my life. And I know it sounds like Pollyanna-ish woo-woo stuff, and maybe it is.

I knew there was only one thing I could control in the maelstrom of life, and that's how I chose to react at any given moment. It took years after Bob1 died for me to learn this lesson, partly because Bob2 entered my life. We managed to surround ourselves with others that had positive outlooks on life and didn't surround themselves with negativity. Say what you want about Amway and other multi-level marketing, but we found ourselves surrounded by people with positive outlooks and learned about communication with different type of people, and the ability to dream of a future untethered by circumstance. When we disconnected from these groups because life got hard and in the way, we found ourselves drawing negative people. I had to make a conscious decision to actively seek out messages of hope, positivity, and growth before Bob died, and certainly after.

Combined with my prior learnings, I moved forward in my grief journey using those principles and doing what I could to help others. I became somewhat of a sage in navigating this course within a few online communities, and then when a fellow parent in town also found herself suddenly single and widowed while working and raising her children, I reached out to offer support, advice and comfort. It's happened a few times in this town, and each time brings me back to that very first Grief Group meeting where I heard, "It gets better" and now I repeat the same thing. Yes, there were times I broke down and cried, either by myself or with my children, because of what they were going to miss, and what Bob was missing in their lives, like our first family vacation.

Before Bob's death, we had planned to return to Family Week in 2014, a week-long celebration of families headed by LGBTQ+ parents in Provincetown. "Are we still allowed to go?" Abby asked.

"Of course we are! Why wouldn't we?"

"Daddy Bob is dead."

"Oh, honey...we are still a family! Remember we talked about all the different kids of families? Some with a mom and a dad, some with two moms or two dads, and some with one mom or one dad, or sometimes aunts, or uncles or grandparents. We're still a family and we are most definitely welcome at Family Week!" I told her.

We had gone with Bob in the summer of 2012, skipping 2013 for Europe. Provincetown was full of memories, including the hours spent at the Cape hospital while Bob was being treated for a DVT. It had only been six months since Bob's death, and I don't know how many times I shared the story with the other parents that I met, and the ones that remembered us from our first time. When the week was nearly over, we had all been emotionally raw, and we cried and held each other for hours. I was reminded, there are no rules for grief, and every emotion when felt is valid and honored.

Those emotions that night most certainly involved anger, and I let the kids know I was angry that he left us and that he left me as a single parent. I let them know THEY could be mad at him just as well—but they could also love him at the same time. They were angry he left them, they were angry because I had different rules, they were angry that I didn't cook like him, and they were angry that I didn't do back to school shopping as well as he did. I was angry because of the way he died, and I resented him for his apparent stupidity. Despite a history of opioid addiction, he allowed his doctors to prescribe for him Fentanyl patches, apparently for pain, on top of a Z-pack for pneumonia. He had accidentally overdosed on his prescribed combination of medicine and became one more statistic in the devastation caused by opioids in America. The more I learned about how the patches worked, the more I wondered if I contributed. Did his body heat spike when I covered him with the blanket and let the dog snuggle with him?

I don't have the answer to that question. I never will, yet I still felt the Survivor's Guilt for many months, maybe even years as I'm recalling this. Was this something I could have changed? I can only think there was no chance for me to have done anything more than what I did. I was torn for a while that my act of kindness in covering him up on a cold January morning could have contributed to his death. I was left wondering if this was the first time he'd gone back to opioids to manage the pain. I was gone so much, would I have noticed? He had a sweet tooth, and the officer that spoke to me while the EMTs were working on him told me that was a sign for addicts. Had that been under my nose all that time?

Some questions will never be answered, and I've tried. I've visited several mediums, one of whom told me that "he didn't want to talk about his death," but there was talk about other parts of our lives together. I had to get myself to a point where I stopped second-guessing myself and him and just accept that I cannot change things out of my control. He was never under my control, and I certainly couldn't do anything to prevent his death. Once I managed to push aside the guilt I felt in not knowing, it was easier to forgive him for making the mistakes he did. And I chose to focus on the good things in our history. I decided to focus on one of the last conversations we had the morning before my flight home.

As most mornings started when I was on the West Coast, we used Skype to check in on each other. This particular morning, he had been up since 2:00am dealing with pneumonia. When I told him I was going to get ready for work and finish packing, he wrote, "OK, babe, have a good day. Love you. Mean it." As I usually do, I replied with a joke, "You too, love you too. Have you been lying?" "No, just haven't said it that way in a while, so I did. And I really do."

That night, Abby had a choral concert at school while I was flying home. Everyone told me he was beaming with pride. That's what I want to remember; that's what I want to hold onto. And I know he loved me. He loved our kids. He loved the home he chose and the community in which we decided to live. I can choose to focus on the bad parts of our life, or I can focus on the love he gave us all. My reaction choices determine my happiness, and I choose to focus on the love given.

## Finding Grateful

With my focus on the positive, I found great joy and positivity in giving back and paying forward to my community. I volunteered with the PTO; this was Bob's realm, so I had the benefit of feeling close to him while helping our students in school. I volunteered to sit on our Town's Architectural Preservation District Commission to maintain the architectural and historical nature of the town center area. I served as an elected official on the School Committee. I provided countless hours of support to other grieving spouses.

When I read an article in our local paper about the Primary School wanting to install a Buddy Bench, I reached out to the school and offered to donate one in Bob's memory. It was red with a plaque donated by the PTO that reads "In Memory of Bob Meek-LaVeck Our Buddy."

I commissioned a song from Tony-Award winning artist Levi Kreis that was inspired by Bob's memory called *"Legacy."* I commissioned a portrait from Michael Volpicelli of Bob made entirely out of words that described him. I did what I could to keep the positive memories alive. Through Levi, I wound up connecting with Del Shores. I eventually became an investor in a film written and directed by Del called *"A Very Sordid Wedding"* that included a photo of Bob, me, and the kids in the end credits. The photo was taken on top of the Notre Dame Cathedral during our Europe trip. Knowing Del and Levi led me to other associations of positive, forward-thinking people. And I shared part of my story with Debby Holiday for her music video *"Waiting For a Lifetime."* These are the people that are my current circle of influence. They ground me, they give unconditional love and support, which I am glad to reciprocate, and they offer an artist's perspective of what can be. This is what I've found I need.

I still participate in some online forums for widowers, primarily to offer some perspective for those experiencing it recently and are lost in the navigation of grief. My advice during the initial months, or even year, is rarely modified:

- Don't listen to anyone else tell you how and when to grieve—this is your journey, not theirs;

- Don't compare your journey. It's yours. It may take you 3 months or 3 years before you choose to do "X," whatever "X" is (move, buy a car, date,etc.). It's all on your comfort and YOUR timeline.

- There is no timeline. You will progress and regress until you die.

- Do what you can to take care of yourself. Drink water, get rest, eat healthily, move. It's easy to fall into bad habits and self-destructive behavior.

- Be prepared for triggers. Every day, every hour, every month, something is going to trigger you. Be prepared. For me, it was simple triggers: At the grocery store, realizing I'm shopping for one; hearing a song on the radio; watching a movie; or, seeing the calendar turn to one of the many days that held meaning to me.

- Anticipate those dates and decide ahead of time how you want to feel that day. If you decide you want to feel sad and cry, then do it. If you decide you want to feel happy with memories, then do it. You choose how you want to celebrate your anniversary or your loved one's birthday. But planning ahead of time lets you think through what you may experience.

- You never get over it. It shapes who you are and what you become. It's easier to manage with time, but it will always be there.

- It does get better over time. At least it feels like it. That's not to say you won't feel sad again. See the next point.

- Grief isn't linear. There's no direct path from anger to acceptance—and once you reach acceptance, you may fall right back into one of the other states of grief. Acceptance, I'm afraid, doesn't mean you are done grieving.

- Feel what you feel when you feel it. Don't stifle emotions; it's unhealthy. Feel it, recognize it, and determine how you want to deal with it. Especially anger. Don't feel guilty about being angry at your loved one. (Though I would suggest not to physically hit things like walls, which can not only damage your wall, but also your hand. I offer this from personal experience. Plus, you may wind up hitting a wall stud. After Bob1 died, I was in the downstairs ¼ bathroom. Angry, sad, likely drunk, when I decided to punch the wall.)

- Don't be afraid to talk about your loved one. It keeps the memory alive and helps to recall positive feelings. If others are uncomfortable talking about your loved one, it's not your problem. It's theirs. You have a right to talk about your loved one.

- Find a way to forgive yourself when you're feeling guilty about something like survivor's guilt.

- There's no stigma in seeking professional help. I can only share what helped me, and part of that journey included professional counseling and grief support groups.

## Conclusion

There's nothing unusual or extraordinarily unique about me. I'm not famous, I haven't cured disease, and I've not been sainted. I'm not a "reality TV" star, a YouTuber or a Social Media Influencer. On the surface, I'm a former West Coast liberal, now an East Coast liberal living in New England. I have two children, a daughter and a son, who are the reason I work so hard. I have two dogs, and I live in a 120-year-old house adorned in red, white, and blue bunting proudly displaying the American flag. I volunteer in the community. I've served on the School Committee and Board of Directors of our Boys and Girls Club. I'm in my mid-fifties with a decidedly typical dad bod, gray hair, and the need to wear reading glasses. To look at me, I'm your average, white, middle-class, single father.

Looking beyond the surface, though, you'll discover that interspersed between the red, white, and blue bunting are bunting in rainbow colors. You'll find that the children I raised and love are not genetically mine, and you'll find that I've managed to do something pretty rare: I had been widowed twice before my 48th birthday.

And here I am, telling you "Yes, there is life after loss."

With focus and an adjustment in your mindset and an understanding of life and grief, you too can move forward with an appreciation for what you have and an appreciation for what you lost. Anyone going through this pain has the tools, or access to the tools, to not only survive it but to find an appreciation of life. I'm an example that it is possible...there IS life after loss and even life after multiple losses. We each have within us the power to define life to be whatever we want it to be. We just need to be ready to do whatever it takes to achieve it. And the good news is, you don't have to do it alone. Lean on your support system, and if you don't have one, make one. Find a local Grief Support Group, join a Facebook Group (there are thousands), go see a licensed counselor. There's an option that will work for you.

I do what I can to enjoy and celebrate life every single day. I try to remind the people I love how much I love them. I can say that I'm more at peace with being a double-widower now and remain in awe of those brave enough to open their hearts for a third, fourth, or even fifth time. And I've seen it many times. Because we grieve, we know we have the capacity to love and be loved. Grief, to me, is proof that I loved.

As a parent, I made the decision to focus on my family and, frankly, what my kids needed, and I suppose to make up for some lost time. As they age, I wonder what my life will be like as an empty-nester. I think of where I want to retire. Sometimes I see an image of someone sharing my life, sometimes I don't. What I do find, regardless, is a vision of a life *I* have chosen to pursue. The future will be here sooner than I think. "Someday" is now.

## Chapter Four
# EPILOGUE

## THE DASH

recall, as I was writing both of the eulogies, a story I'd heard about a tombstone and mourners looking at the dates. When I first heard Sally tell me that John's memorial was going to be celebration of his life, and not a mourning of his death, it became clear to me the importance of the mark in between the birth date and the death date. And, while it didn't come out until after John and Bob1 had both passed away, I later found the poem *"The Dash"* by Linda Ellis.

It inspired me to live between those dates. Live your life within those dates.

### The Dash
*the poem by Linda Ellis*

*I read of a man who stood to speak at the funeral of a friend. He referred to the dates on the tombstone from the beginning... to the end.*
*He noted that first came the date of birth and spoke of the following date with tears, but he said what mattered most of all was the dash between those years.*

*For that dash represents all the time they
spent alive on earth and now only those who
loved them know what that little line is worth.*

*For it matters not, how much we own,
the cars... the house... the cash. What matters
is how we live and love and how we spend
our dash.*

*So think about this long and hard; are
there things you'd like to change? For you
never know how much time is left that still can
be rearranged.*

*To be less quick to anger and show
appreciation more and love the people in our
lives like we've never loved before.*

*If we treat each other with respect and
more often wear a smile... remembering that
this special dash might only last a little while.*

*So when your eulogy is being read, with
your life's actions to rehash, would you be
proud of the things they say about how you
lived your dash?*

*By Linda Ellis, Copyright © 2020 Inspire Kindness,
thedashpoem.com*

## 7 Years Later

Our children are older now, Abby is a beautiful 18-year-old
with long, very curly, very dark brown hair. Her green eyes

are now hazel, framed by expressive eyebrows and freckles on her cheeks. Daniel is in-between boy and man, and at 17- years-old, he's closer to the man side of that spectrum. He fits into Daddy Bob's old work shoes with his thin frame. The wild hair he had when I first met him has been tamed, and his face has little in common with the baby face I first fell in love with.

They're good kids, kids that I know Bob Meek-LaVeck would be proud of and proud to show off. I cried many tears during those moments he physically missed, whether it was Abby's vocal concerts, basketball games, or high school graduation, or Daniel's moving into high school, taking driver's education or riding the mower in the yard the first time.

I recognize he started them on their paths in life as the stay-at-home parent, and while my methods may be different and I may not have done some things the same way, they had a good foundation. I see some of him in them, and he remains very much a part of our family life.

I believe he's still watching over them, for what parent wouldn't?

## 25 Years Later

I've lived in this Massachusetts house since June 2011, and I have never seen a hummingbird in this yard. Ever. 25 years ago, as Bob suffered through a particularly bad period of chemotherapy, we saw a yellow bird land in the palm tree in the back yard. He had literally just said he no longer saw the joy in living, but he saw that bird and said it gave him joy.

After he died, I always saw a hummingbird in the yard. When I'd think of him, or speak to him, this hummingbird would appear.

Today, August 14, 2020, I was working out at the park and I saw a yellow bird. It being the 25th anniversary of his passing, I thought of Bob Roders and that yellow bird of the past and smiled.

Later that afternoon, Daniel and I were enjoying the pool and I noticed a yellow bird land in the garden. I watched it for a moment, feasting on the insects, and went back to swimming. Moments later, a hummingbird appeared at the door, then went to the side of the pool, then around the other side before it disappeared.

Signs. I believe they were signs and a message that he's still with me, 25 years later.

## Chapter Five

# ACKNOWLEDGMENTS

## SHARING THE MUSIC

I wanted to take a few pages to share the songs (the full liner notes) and artists that were part of the tape series I did, as well as the song by Levi Kreis. Music is universal and readily available and I find many times far more expressive than I.

## *Tape I–The "Grief is Killing Me" Tape*
**Music For Robert–Volume I**
**Memorial Music Selections–February 1996**

"The Song Remembers When" things were different. I chose this forum to express my emotional loss with Bob's death because everywhere I turn, I hear songs that, for some reason or another, remind me of better times with him. Songs that make me smile or cry. Mostly cry.

It is because of these songs that I cannot and do not want to forget those better times. And I am sharing these with you.

There were so many songs I wanted to put on this cassette, but the tape wasn't long enough! So, I decided that this would be Volume I. Volume II will be worked on later and maybe there will even be a Volume III or IV. With the wealth of music pouring over the airwaves, I am sure there are more songs that are there, waiting for me to hear.

I chose music from many different categories: country, rock, R&B, pop, oldies. I am sure that as you listen to the words of these songs, by the artists who performed them, you will understand why that particular song was chosen to help me express those emotions.

So, sit back, close your eyes, listen and enjoy...

### The Dance–Performed by Garth Brooks

I chose this song for obvious reasons: the emotions it evokes reminds me of the good times we had. It reminds me that I wouldn't have given up any of it because, if I did, I'd have missed the Dance of our lives. I had this song played at Bob's memorial service, and parts quoted in the obituary. Everyone I talked to said that it is beautiful and reminds them that they were part of that Dance, too.

### Since You've Been Gone–Performed by High Strung

Though time is beginning to make it a little easier for me to deal with Bob's death, I still feel "scared and lost and all alone" since he's been gone. I found this song quite by accident, as a selection on the monthly New Country CD I get, and I was immediately drawn to it.

### Where Do You Start?–Performed by Michael Feinstein

I've always liked this song since I first heard it several years ago. Though it seems to be more of a "break-up" song, I find that it can easily be translated into dealing with the loss of a loved one. "Where do you start? How do you separate the present from the past?" These are questions I've been asking myself and others since August 1995.

### In This Life–Performed by Bette Midler

Bette Midler brings such passion to this song. Though I've heard it for years on country radio by another artist, it wasn't until I lost Bob and heard this version that I really got it: the only dream that ever mattered had come true in this life, I was loved by him. I cried my eyes out, realizing that sharing love is what matters most.

### I Will Remember You–Performed by Amy Grant

It seems like everywhere I turn, I see Bob or have a memory of things we used to do or did. Sitting here typing, I can remember how he'd come up behind me and put his hands on my shoulders while I was at the computer. If I close my eyes, I can almost feel his hands...

### Inside of Me–Performed by Madonna

Regardless of the tempo and the overt sexuality of Madonna's singing on this song, I chose it because of the words. I will always have a part of Bob inside of me, in my heart. He's part of who I am (it's his fault).

### Unforgettable–by Natalie and Nat "King" Cole

Natalie Cole was able to "sing" with her father after his death on this song. Bob is completely Unforgettable in his own right. I wish I could sing with him again. He and I used to sing "Unforgivable, that's what you are ..."

### *In The Wee Small Hours of The Morning–Performed by Carly Simon*

When I wake up in those wee small hours of the morning, around 1 or 2 am (which is often), "that's the time I miss him most of all." I was so used to his being there, never imagining that he wouldn't be.

### *If I Could Only Stay Asleep–Performed by Patsy Cline*

Bob was a Patsy Cline fan and this song reflects much of what I'm going through. I like the dreams I've had (mostly) because I can spend time with him. If I could only stay asleep, I'd be with him always.

### *Goodbye My Friend–Performed by Linda Ronstadt*

I lost my best friend on August 14, 1995. Bob was more than a lover, a companion, a husband, whatever. He was my best friend—someone I could always count on. Someone I could tell anything to. I miss the friendship most of all, I think. Goodbye, my friend, you are missed...

### *How Can I Help You Say Goodbye–Performed by Patty Loveless*

I admit I wasn't fond of this song when I first heard it a few years ago, but now I can appreciate the emotional level of loss expressed. I guess we all have to say "goodbye" eventually, and Bob at least had the opportunity to tell his friends and family (including the surrogate family of LaVecks and Medveds) goodbye. I guess he even helped me to say goodbye to him, though it wasn't easy. It isn't easy.

**Can't Be Really Gone–Performed by Tim McGraw**

If you substitute the gender specific "she" with "he" then you'll be able to see why I included this song. Looking around the house, there are many of Bob's things around—it's almost like he's coming back, that he "can't be really gone." Of course, I know that's not going to happen no matter how much I want it to.

**Everything Must Change–Performed by Oleta Adams**

It's true, "everything must change, nothing stays the same." Death is a part of life and, like it or not, life changes as the seasons change. We each have our Springs, our Falls, our Summers and our Winters. I'm now in a Winter and Spring will eventually come.

**(Without You) What Do I Do With Me?–Performed by Tanya Tucker**

This is a question I've asked many times. What's next? What do I do with me now? Eventually, I'll find the answers. Right now, I don't know. "I don't want to go out, but I just can't stay home;" don't want to eat, but I have to. Everything seems to be a Catch-22—damned if I do and damned if I don't.

**The Rose–Performed by Bette Midler**

I picked this song because it reminds me of a time when Bob and I were at a friend's house in Santa Barbara. It was Bobby Gerard's house and he was hosting a "gathering" with John Payne in attendance. John was a great person: funny, charming, talented, friendly. John was playing this song on the piano and he and I were singing (I tried the harmony). John was a great friend who passed away a few years ago. I know that he and Bob are together in heaven and having fun.

### With This Tear–Performed by Celine Dion

You have to listen carefully to hear the words which is unfortunate (thank God for CD covers with lyrics!). Basically, the song is about someone who is dealing with the loss of a loved one who promised never to leave, but who told her that he was dying. I've cried many tears over the last year and, with each one, I want him back more and more. We cried many tears together. "With this tear, I thee want. I long for you to talk to me like you did that night in the restaurant..." I remember for our 6th anniversary, right before we bought the house, we went to a nice restaurant to celebrate. I asked him to "mortgage me" and he accepted.

### Tears in Heaven–Performed by Eric Clapton

Eric Clapton wrote this song after the tragic death of his young son. I wasn't crazy about this one either when I first heard it. Now I understand: There is no room for tears in heaven.

### The One–Performed by Elton John

When you find the one, you know it. Bob was definitely the one for me. He took me as I was, with faults and all. It's a rare thing to find someone to share your life with, someone that accepts everything about you. I was lucky. I must have done something right. He didn't want me to be alone after he died and maybe, someday, I'll find someone who will accept me with all the baggage I've got...

### *Angel–Performed by Jon Secada*

I believe Bob is my Guardian Angel (or, as I told him, my Gardening Angel). I'm sure he's an Angel in heaven, watching over all of us. He was an Angel on Earth and, as was said at his service, "Heaven is a much better place now with him there."

### *Yesterday–Performed by Billy Dean*

Paul McCartney wrote this song after his mother's death. I remember happier times, in Santa Barbara, with friends, in that funky house, with the dogs. I think a lot about our yesterdays. All our troubles seemed so far away.

### *The Song Remembers When–Performed by Trisha Yearwood*

Usually, when I least expect it, something will remind me of the time we had and the dreams that will never come true. Most of the time, it's a song that puts me in that place, that remembers when things were different...

### *Go Rest High On That Mountain–Performed by Vince Gill*

Vince Gill wrote this song for his brother. This is a beautiful song. I pray that Bob rests in peace since he no longer has the problems of this world.

## Tape II–The "Attitude" Tape
**Music For Robert–Volume II**
**Memorial Music Selections–June 1996**

I certainly can't say that the last several months have been easy or even remotely enjoyable. What has been nice were the comments I received from so many who received tapes of Volume I.

The comments ranged from the tape being a beautiful tribute, to causing crying to a bit melancholy – though I can't imagine it being anything but.

I have worked on this volume for the past four months, since the first volume was completed in February 1996. And, each time I thought I had all the songs I needed, I heard another and thought, "I must add that to the mix."

So, here we have Volume II (with several left over for Volume III). I know that some of you may again have tears, or smiles or think that I am being too depressing and melancholic. You'll notice that the music is also a bit of a different mix. You'll probably also think that it is tinged with attitude (which is probably correct). However, that is how I am feeling. I continue to fight the urge to stay under the covers and remain at home, never to leave. I tend only to travel to and from work and to and from the bereavement support group. Socializing is still difficult for me, seeing other couples smiling and laughing. Bob was the social butterfly, always able to enjoy himself (even at my work functions where he knew no one).

He touched so many lives and was such a huge chunk of mine: my buddy, my friend, my life, my love.

So, in the meantime, I continue to escape through the sounds of the music...

### *Crippled Bird—Dolly Parton*

Sometimes, I feel like that crippled bird with a broken wing. The wing will heal and the bird will take flight again. And, just as my heart has been broken by Bob's death, it too shall heal and it shall fly again. I realize, of course, that it will take time. Please listen to all of the words, not just the chorus.

### *I Wish I Didn't Love You So—kd lang*

Bob and I have always been great fans of kd lang. One of our Sunday rituals was to get the morning paper, crawl under the covers with a pot of coffee next to us, and watch the recorded Saturday Night Live from the prior evening. That is how we first learned of kd lang and the incredible power of her voice. I've always liked this song and it seems appropriate to the mood of this cassette. It would be easier to get on with my life if I didn't love him so much.

### *Wish You Were Here–Michael Feinstein*

Nothing seems to be the same during this year after Bob died. The leaves are the wrong color, as is the sky. The days just don't seem to have the same joy as before (not that life was always a bed of roses). And I have made the wish many times that he were here. But I realize that things will always be different for me now.

### Man of My Word–Collin Raye

I made a promise of love and now it cannot be returned
to me. The Promise at times does feel like a prison, I still
feel "married." Logically, I know that the Promise should
no longer matter, that I can break that Promise and go
forward. But my heart just can't seem to allow me to accept
the truth at this time.

### What Do They Know–Tanya Tucker

Many people have told me what I should do to get on with
my life, and I appreciate their concern and I know they mean
well. However, as the saying goes, unless you've walked a
mile in my shoes... I have to heal and grieve at my own pace.
These tapes are part of that process. I guess this song has
some attitude, but it's appropriate for the mood on this tape.

### Busy Being Blue–kd lang

I have had many excuses to avoid being in social
situations—"I'm busy in the yard, gotta wash the dog, bad
hair day..." But I'm really just too busy being blue.

### Guess I'll Hang My Tears Out To Dry/In The Wee Small Hours of the Morning–Frank Sinatra and Carly Simon

I was thinking of adding this song to the first tape, but the
Carly Simon version was more appropriate for that tape.
Guess I'll have to hang my teardrops out to dry eventually...

### I'll Never Stop Loving You–Cher

It seems as though I heard these words from Bob's mouth
just days before he died. We spent many hours talking

about the last 7 years of our lives together, the good, the bad, the ugly. We forgave each other for any grievances caused because we knew we never stopped loving each other.

### *Who Turned Out The Light–Kathy Mattea*

Someone turned out the light of our relationship. Who decided we weren't meant to be? I've questioned a lot of things over the last several months, my faith being one of those. Just when things were going well, our lives were bright, someone turned out the light and left me in the dark to fumble for the light switch.

### *Wish That I Could Tell You–Reba McIntyre*

I really didn't know how to help him say goodbye. All I could do was be there for him, and that didn't seem to be enough, though I'm sure it was. I also wish that I could have told him many things that weigh heavy on me now, my fears and doubts about his leaving me. Instead, I kept the "stiff upper lip" and tried to be "strong," which I think was more of a mistake than anything else. Of course, I didn't know any better.

### *A Bad Goodbye–Clint Black with Wynonna*

I really didn't think this song was appropriate at first until I heard Clint Black sing it solo. It changed in my mind and didn't seem to be such a break-up song. Bob wanted to make sure that I was okay before he said goodbye, he didn't want to leave me with a bad goodbye.

### *Dreaming My Dreams With You–Collin Raye*

It seems that all of the dreams I had included Bob and our life together. Those dreams haven't changed: they have simply died along with Bob. Those dreams no longer exist and I am forced to make new dreams for myself, alone. I will always miss dreaming my dreams with him.

### *Trying to Get Over You–Vince Gill*

Believe it or not, I am trying to get on with my life. I have spent some time with good friends, spoken to others after months of silence. Little baby steps...

### *It's Not the End of the World–Emilio*

I know it's not the end of the world, my heart keeps beating, the sun keeps rising, life continues. I'm not sure how these things continue, but they do.

### *When The Thought Of You Catches Up With Me– David Ball*

It still happens, I can be doing something and have a memory that stops me in my tracks. Memories of times past, when things were so much different.

### *My Buddy–Dr. John*

A friend at work found this song for me. I miss my buddy, the sound of his voice, the touch of his hand...

### *Just Get One–Ty Herndon with Vince Gill*

I have learned, over these last few months, that Bob and I shared so much with each other, that we were truly in love, that we meant so much to each other. But our stubbornness sometimes got in the way. You don't really know what you have until either you're about to lose it, or you have lost it.

### I Will Always Love You–Dolly Parton with Vince Gill

I've had several occasions where I feel there has been a "visitation." Sometimes, I'll talk to Bob and something will happen to remind me that he is there. Once, I was talking to him, asking THE question I've been asking for months, "Why did you leave me?" All of a sudden, I heard this song playing from the TV and I wept because I was sure Bob was speaking to me.

### Because You Loved Me–Celine Dion

I've already blamed Bob for how I am, but that was always in jest. He was always there for me when I needed him, as I was for him. It is simply because he loved me, that I'm everything I am.

### Have I Told You Lately?–Emilio

This song was a bonus I found on the CD. I didn't know it was there! During the second week or so of the chemotherapy, the doctor decided that Bob needed a spinal tap and injection of chemo into the spinal column. I went with him to the hospital while this was done, awake, on a bed. I held his hand while he was curled in a fetal position. This song (the Rod Stewart version) started playing over the hospital music system. Bob squeezed my hand harder, mouthed the words to the song, and cried. I tried to be "strong," but cried silently to myself.

### *Stay Forever–Hal Ketchum*

I heard this song a lot when Bob was sick. Maybe I did pray too much, wasting God's time, but I was sure that if He could see how much love there was, Bob would be able to stay with me forever. I think Bob stayed as long as he did after they sent him home because of the love we shared, thinking it would be enough to keep him here. But it wasn't.

### *How Do You Keep The Music Playing?/Funny Valentine–Frank Sinatra and Lorrie Morgan*

How do you keep the music playing, the music of two hearts beating in unison, the music of life and love?

### *The Last Song–Elton John*

While Bob lay on his bed, withering from the destruction of his body, he told us that he had several experiences. He told us he walked with his mother (a woman who died over 20 years ago who could barely walk), he said he saw Christ, and he saw God. One of the biggest questions on his mind, and I would guess it's a question we all ask, was "Where do I go now? And will God accept me in heaven?" I hear this song and I imagine that the Father is God, coming for his son.

### *Il Sogno di Volare–Cirque du Soleil*

When Bob worked at Stampa Barbara, the owner of the store took his staff and guests to see Cirque du Soleil in Santa Monica. Bob and I went and were completely enthralled in the performance. This piece was playing during an extremely graceful trapeze act. We loved the music so much, we bought the CD. This music was playing at 11:35am, Monday, August 14, 1995 when Bob died. To me, this is the last song.

Submitted to you, with love and thanks for the love and continued support you have given me.

## Tape III–The "Hopeful" Tape
**Music For Robert–Volume III**
**Memorial Music Selections–February 1997**

I can't believe it has been a year since Volume I! Once again, you'll notice a different attitude on this, the final tape of the series. I do not anticipate a Volume IV. And, you will also notice a variety of music and artists, many of whom you have heard before.

The last 18 months has been a growth experience that I would have given anything not to have gone through. But, since I didn't have a choice in the matter, I had to get through it somehow.

There were many days when getting out of bed didn't seem appealing to me. There are still a few of those days, but I believe for the most part, my damaged heart and soul are healing. I have actually socialized with people instead of hiding in our home.

I don't mean to say that I am better. I am getting stronger, I know that I must continue forward with my life, as Bob would want, and that the last year and a half has not been easy for me. My good friends, my loving, supportive family, my bereavement support group: these things have been my rock, my strength. I am forever grateful for these people in my life.

I'm not sure anyone has noticed it, but there is a chronology and deliberate placement of the songs on these cassettes. Just thought you'd like to know. Once again, the sounds of music...

### The Wind–Mariah Carey

It seems as though the wind has taken Bob, just blew through and took him with it, so that he could be free of pain and at peace at last. Though he was still much too young to die.

### Fly–Celine Dion

Last time, it was a crippled bird learning to fly again. And with the wind, Bob has had a chance to fly, beyond the planets and the stars. Mom and I told him that he was just going before us so that he could save us a window seat. His endless journey has begun.

### Unchained Melody–LeAnn Rimes

I can't help but think of the movie Ghost when I hear this song. And, when I think of ghosts, I think of death and, when I think of death, I think of Bob (see, there is some semblance of a thought process in my mind). LeAnn Rimes' voice is just so haunting on this version of the song and in listening to the words, it appears appropriate to this tape.

### *Where Are You Now?–Clint Black*

The death of a loved one can leave the survivors to question things they have been told all their lives. I have certainly questioned a lot of things over the last two years and, after Bob died, I questioned where he was. I'm still not quite sure what happens or where we go when we die. I only know that in the end, it will happen to us all. Then I'll know. But for now, there's that burning question on my mind for Bob.

### *You Know How I Feel–Bryan White*

Empathy is a difficult thing to master and nearly impossible for those whose experiences are different. One can have sympathy for someone who has lost their spouse, but true empathy, true understanding, comes with the shared experience. I wouldn't wish this experience on anyone, it's not fun. But there are certain things that everyone experiences sooner or later, some of them are listed in this song, and if you've experienced part of what I have, then you know how I feel. Of course, I know how you feel – you lost Bob, too.

### *If Blue Tears Were Silver–Jon Randall*

So many tears have been cried. What's the old saying, "If I had a nickel for every…"? It's true, if my tears were silver and my memories gold, I'd be a very rich person. However, material possessions only mean so much when you can't share them with the right person. And my memories are more treasured than anything that gold or silver can buy.

### *To Be Forgiven–George Michael*

I have felt like I've been drowning. I know that the river has taken me places I didn't want to go. This song hit a chord for some reason. Maybe because the house we bought was near a river, maybe because I felt I needed saving, maybe because I'd beg to be forgiven, if I knew my sin.

### *Thinkin' About You–Trisha Yearwood*

So many times, I just sit back, literally, and think of Bob and the time we spent together. Sometimes, I think of times when it was just the two of us. Other times, I remember parties with crowds and tuxedos, quiet dinners with close friends, trips taken, margarita-induced munchies of chips and salsa. Seems like anything I try to do, or anything I see in the house, still brings back a lot of memories. They don't depress me like they used to, though. Sometimes, I'll catch myself laughing out loud.

### *Home Alone–4 Runner*

The house really does seem empty since I've been home alone. I even rented out a room in the house, but that's not even close.

### *Ever Since I Lost Your Love–Cliff Eberhardt*

Things are the same in the world, but not really. A lot of it is just in going through the motions. It's the same old life, except that Bob is gone and not in it.

### *Still Life–Bryan White*

What a wonderful play on words! It's like a painting, a still life, and it's still life without Bob.

### Tell Me–Go West

I know that Bob's leaving didn't have anything to do with me – it wasn't anything I did wrong, but still, a part of me wonders if there was anything else I could have done to prevent this.

### What Becomes of The Broken Hearted–Paul Young

You know, I have often wondered what becomes of those whose hearts have been broken. Mine was not only broken but beaten and battered senseless, left to heal at whatever rate it takes to heal such injury to such an important organ.

### That's Another Song–Bryan White

It's another song, and you've already heard three hours full of music that explain this fact. It really is amazing how I miss the little things that Bob did, some endearing and some just plain annoying. Even as I sort laundry, I miss the fact that his clothes aren't there anymore.

### Before There Was You–Ty Herndon

I have to say that I really didn't exist in the right way before I met Bob. I never really felt like a "whole" person. He was a one-winged angel that I latched onto so that we could fly together. Now, my one wing is getting tired but I'm going to need to get used to flying solo for awhile.

### If I Were You–Terri Clark

I heard this song last year, and thought of adding it to Volume I. That Volume was done around Valentine's Day, the day for love and lovers. At work, those that didn't get flowers from their mates griped about that fact. I just thought, "You know, at least you have someone at home that loves you." So, to all those that take what they have for granted, I remind them that they shouldn't do so.

### *Can't Run From Yourself–Tanya Tucker*
Bob and I always liked this song. And, the truth of the matter is, you can't run from yourself. I'm learning to tackle the problems head-on. I tried running and everything else to avoid being in the realm of humanity, but I just can't run from myself.

### *Now I Know–Lari White*
I didn't always wonder what I'd do without Bob. I don't really think I had thoughts like that while he was still with me. I guess the fact that I'm still here 18 months later says that I'm strong enough to make it on my own, I'm learning how to face it alone. Though I'd still prefer not to.

### *I Didn't Know My Own Strength–Lorrie Morgan*
I knew I was strong – always tried to give Bob the strength to fight, always hid my fears and concern (though I didn't do such a good job hiding anything, he knew me just too damn well). After he left, I was lost. I didn't know what to do. I did things that I had to do to stay on schedule and I pretty much did everything by rote. I didn't think my strength would see me through this. I guess I was wrong.

### *There Isn't One–Linda Davis*
I've tried many things to forget, to move on: avoidance, drinking too much, eating too much, smoking too much,

working too much, hiding in the house, working on the yard, support groups, these tapes, writing, crying, sharing. I think I've tried many things, but the non-self-destructive steps and efforts have had the best results.

### All By Myself–Eric Carmen

It's hard to believe that next month, I would have known Bob 9 years and in July, we would have celebrated our 9th anniversary! I was much younger then, as was he. Things certainly were different...

### In Between Dances–Pam Tillis

If my time with Bob was The Dance, then I guess I'm just between dances right now, sitting it out for awhile. I know he wanted me to Dance again someday. It's just that it's been nearly 10 years since I've Danced with anyone else. I'm not sure I know the steps anymore.

### Move On–George Michael

This is just one of those songs that hit me between the eyes. I have seen things I never wanted to see. I wrote before on Volume I about the seasons of our lives, and there's a verse in this song about waiting for that change of season, the Winter's been so long. The funny thing about seasons, though, is that they don't last forever. I guess I need to get back on my feet...to move on.

Well, that's it. I'm not going to say that life is great and that I like where I'm at now in my life. I will say that I have managed to take some steps toward healing, and the hurt, while still very much alive, is not all-consuming anymore. I know the hurt will never leave, and I am beginning to learn how to live with it instead of for it. Yeah, I'm getting better. I think I can do it.

Once again, submitted to you, with love and thanks for the love and continued support you have given me.

## Legacy–By Levi Kreis

### *Legacy*

*Song Commission Written by Levi Kreis–August 2015*

I knew a man
He had a smile like the sunrise
A sweetness in his eyes
And open arms
He always said
This time here is borrowed
Don't wait 'til tomorrow
To make your mark
'Cause there's someone out there waiting to believe
And what you got to give may be the very thing they need
(Ch.)
So flash a little smile
Show a little kindness
Give a little love along the way
Hug a little tighter
Shine a little brighter
Be the one to make it a better day
Take a little time to make a difference

And soon you're gonna see
That love is gonna be your legacy
Days like these
I think about what he gave us
The memories that made us
The years of our love
What I now know
Is to pay it all forward
To carry it over
To someone else
Cause when everything we touch just fades away
Love is gonna be the only thing that remains
Ch.
Love lives on
In the eyes of the children
In the words of a good friend
In a stranger's smile
Love is forever
When we give to each other
It's bigger than you and me
Ch.

# ABOUT THE AUTHOR

James LaVeck (www.jameslaveck.com) has spent the greater part of his life consulting for financial institutions and providing project management services. He has helped produce two movies and a classical-crossover album. He is also an author and wrote his memoir, *Life After Losses.*

Jim fell in love with his first husband, Bob, and spent seven years with him before losing him. After a number of years, and with much struggle, he got back to himself and began to date again. He married his second husband and lost him, as well.

He began to write his memoir as a cathartic exercise, but it began to metamorphose into a profound narrative that addressed the human experience in learning to deal with the loss of a significant other.

With his deep and personal story, he has penned what it's like to feel intense passion towards someone, building a life together, raising children, and dealing with an overbearing sense of grief.

He is a native Californian who currently resides in Massachusetts with his two teenage children and two dogs. He enjoys music, musical theatre, and movies. He enjoys going to concerts and is at present learning to play the piano.

After several years of volunteering in the community, he has also begun to take acting classes and vocal lessons with the hope of participating in community theatre projects.

CPSIA information can be obtained
at www.ICGtesting.com
Printed in the USA
LVHW092258080221
678696LV00003B/32